Kierkegaard's Philosophy

Self-Deception and Cowardice in the Present Age

John Douglas Mullen

University Press of America, Inc.
Lanham • New York • London

Copyright © 1995 by
University Press of America,® Inc.
4720 Boston Way
Lanham, Maryland 20706

3 Henrietta Street
London, WC2E 8LU England

Library of Congress Cataloging-in-Publication Data
is available from the publisher.

EITHER/OR, by Søren Kierkegaard, Vol. I, translated by David F.
Swenson and Lillian Marvin Swenson, and Vol. II, translated by
Walter Lowrie, both with Revisions and Foreword by Howard A.
Johnson, and both copyright 1944 © 1959 by Howard A. Johnson,
Princeton Paperback, 1971. FEAR AND TREMBLING and THE
SICKNESS UNTO DEATH, by Søren Kierkegaard, translated by
Walter Lowrie (copyright 1941, 1954 by Princeton University Press,
Princeton Paperback, 1968); THE CONCEPT OF DREAD, by Søren
Kierkegaard, translated by Walter Lowrie (copyright 1944 © 1957 by
Princeton University Press, Princeton Paperback, 1967); TWO AGES:
THE AGE OF REVOLUTION and THE PRESENT AGE: A
LITERARY REVIEW, by Søren Kierkegaard, ed. and translated by
Howard V. Hong and Edna H. Hong (copyright ©1978 by Howard V.
Hong) (Kierkegaard's Writings XIV), published by Princeton
University Press. CONCLUDING UNSCIENTIFIC POSTSCRIPT, by
Søren Kierkegaard, translated by David F. Swenson and Walter
Lowrie (copyright 1941 ©1969 by Princeton University Press),
published for the American Scandinavian Foundation: Reprinted by
permission of Princeton University Press.

ISBN 0-8191-9803-X (pbk.: alk. paper)

ACKNOWLEDGMENTS

I wish to acknowledge the inspiration of Michael Martin and the late Theodore Mischel, who were in many ways models to me of philosophical clarity and integrity. The late Gregor Malantschuk, by his unequaled Kierkegaard scholarship, and by his gracious encouragement during that all-too-brief time that I knew him, was indispensible to this work. And finally I would acknowledge the assistance of my friend James O. Tate, who affected this work in ways that neither of us are fully aware. There is one other, Constance Mullen, whose contribution to my life and thought can never be recorded.

For John and Florence Mullen
with Love and Gratitude

CONTENTS

LIST OF KIERKEGAARD'S WRITINGS

Below is a list of Kierkegaard's major works in English in the order of their composition. The abbreviations used in this book are indicated to the left of the English title.

[CI]   *The Concept of Irony* (1841), Indiana University Press, 1965

[E/O]   *Either/Or*, vols. I, II (1843), Princeton University Press, 1959

[ED]   *Edifying Discourses*, vols. I-IV (1843-4), Augsburg Publishing, 1946.

[FT]   *Fear and Trembling* (1843), Princeton University Press, 1954

[R]   *Repetition* (1843), Harper Torchbooks, 1941

[PF]   *Philosophical Fragments* (1844), Princeton University Press, 1962

[CD]   *Concept of Dread* (1844), Princeton University Press, 1954

[SLW]   *Stages on Life's Way* (1845), Schocken Books, 1967

[CUP]   *Concluding Unscientific Postscript* (1846), Princeton University Press, 1941

[TA]   *Two Ages* (1846), Princeton University Press, 1978

[GA]   *Of the Difference Between a Genius and an Apostle* (1847), Harper Torchbooks, 1962

[PH]   *Purity of Heart* (1847), Harper Torchbooks, 1956

[GS]   *The Gospel of Suffering* (1847), Augsburg Publishing, 1948

[WL]   *Works of Love* (1847), Harper Torchbooks, 1962

[ChD]   *Christian Discourses* (1848), Princeton University Press, 1971

[CLA]   *Crisis in the Life of an Actress* (1848), Harper Torchbooks, 1967

[SUD]   *The Sickness unto Death* (1849), Princeton University Press, 1968.

[TC]   *Training in Christianity* (1850), Princeton University Press, 1944

[PV]   *The Point of View for My Work as an Author* (1851), Harper Torchbooks, 1962

[SE]   *For Self-Examination and Judge for Yourself* (1851), Princeton University Press, 1944

[AC]   *Attack upon "Christendom"* (1854-55), Princeton University Press, 1968

[LD]   *Kierkegaard: Letters and Documents*, Princeton University Press, 1978

[J&P]   *Søren Kierkegaard's Journals and Papers*, vols. I-VII, Indiana University Press, 1967-78

KIERKEGAARD'S PHILOSOPHY

INTRODUCTION

Søren Kierkegaard was a towering genius of the nineteenth century. More clearly than anyone else he understood the shape of modernity, that malaise from which we now suffer. During his lifetime, the modern assumptions of "the present age" were still restricted to the vanguard; today they have infiltrated every aspect of our lives. It is for this reason that we are in greater need of Kierkegaard's wisdom today than were his contemporaries. Yet, although Kierkegaard planted himself in direct opposition to modern forms of thought, it would be a terrible error to approach his work as that of a social critic. Søren Kierkegaard was a philosopher of the human spirit. To come to understand what he is saying is to be challenged *as a person*. The challenge is in the form of an interrogation, the topic of which is very simple: You are an existing person, a human being; do you treat this fact with the seriousness and respect it demands? Or would you rather avoid the question? Let me explain.

There are many kinds of philosophers who set for themselves many sorts of tasks. One way to divide the territory is to think of how near to, or far from, the everyday life of the individual person a philosopher's thoughts are. That is, to think of what would be the consequences to the individual person of having adopted the views of this or that philosopher.

If we look at philosophers in this way, we have a spectrum. At one end are the great philosophical systems of

1

Aristotle, Leibniz, Whitehead, and Carnap, as examples. Their concerns range beyond the life of the individual to such abstract areas as natural philosophy, political theory, and the foundations of logic and science. No one familiar with the history of western culture can deny the importance and the influence of this type of philosophy. But you, the individual, experience its effects only indirectly. They touch your life only after having been filtered through the social institutions of science, religion, politics, and the academic disciplines.

At the other end of the spectrum are the great "insight" philosophers who speak in direct and concrete terms to the worries, fears, myths, and values of everyday life. Examples here would include Epictetus, Nietzsche, Camus, and Simone Weil. It is not that this type of philosophy ignores the more general and abstract questions, but it deals with them only insofar as is necessary in order to clarify an issue concerning concrete, everyday, individual life. The question of the spectrum is one of focus and degree: the degree to which you, the individual, can directly incorporate the philosophy of an author into the center of your life.

Confusion concerning this spectrum has often led people who are in search of personal insight to inquire in the wrong places. Believing that philosophers are thinkers of wisdom, and that wisdom is what is needed, a person may decide to challenge the fascinating, but in this case unsatisfying, complexities of Leibniz's *Monadology*. While this work is a brilliant and important piece of philosophy, its concerns are those of seventeenth-century metaphysics and not the philosophical issues of everyday life. In like manner, readers who bring their own anxieties to the study of Freud's *The Problem of Anxiety* will be left unmoved. It is true that the history of western philosophy contains what wisdom our culture has been able to produce, and it is doubly true that wisdom is what is most lacking in the life of the individual today, but one must know where and how to find it.

This problem of where and how to look has led many others in the direction of charlatans, and has spawned an entire industry devoted to the production of uncritical, superficial drivel about "how to live your life." The "pop psych" or "self-help" section of your bookstore, as well as the racks at the supermarket, are bulging with this literature. Its authors can be seen dispensing their personalities on the afternoon talk shows. I call it drivel because it never asks you to look at the fundamentals which underlie your life. If you have read any of this material, the chances are that you were searching for something. Perhaps you were not clear as to the object of your search; perhaps you haven't thought about it. This popular-therapy literature promises an end to your search by recommending some minor adjustment, by providing some superficial insight wrapped in catchy phrases, or by suggesting a list of exercises, whether physical, meditative, social, psychological, or dietary. What all this has in common is the assumption that your life has no depth; that what you need and are searching for is resting there on the surface of the everyday. This, though, is not true. And that fact is not something about which you should be worried. You need not be a "neurotic" person to have needs which have depth and complexity, you need only be a *real* person. But despite its superficiality, this popular-therapy literature does have a virtue, one which accounts no doubt for its wide appeal. The virtue is that it speaks directly and in concrete terms to the life of the individual person. While it fails to provide satisfactory answers, at least it asks some of the right questions. It holds out promise.

A characteristic of wisdom is that it drives toward the concerns which lie at the center of a question. Beginning with the everyday, it leads one to the profound, and then back again. Having returned to the everyday, one is in a position to apply the lessons of the journey. The key, then, is to speak directly and concretely to the life of the individual as he lives it, but to speak with wisdom. This is the task which Søren Kierkegaard adopted, and it is this which he does better than almost any other philosopher. I will state categorically that no one, not the most ordinary person nor the most sophisticated and blasé intellectual, can even begin to understand what Kierkegaard was doing in his writing without being profoundly influenced by him. Kierkegaard challenges his reader, almost taunts him, to avoid living as a fool and as a coward. He was a great admirer of Socrates, and was of course aware of the Socratic dictum "Know thyself." And he agreed that nothing could be more important. But Kierkegaard noticed something which the Greek in Socrates prevented him from seeing: that people often *choose not* to know themselves. His task was to help others in their search. But he knew that this meant not only to provide some new ideas, but also to induce his reader to let down his defenses. The problem, therefore, was not only one of knowledge but also one of will. The point was not only to instruct but to deliver. Using Plato's analogy, the task was not only to show his reader the way out of the cave (of self-ignorance) but to give him the courage to leave.

When you are inclined to say of someone that he is a fool, it is usually because he appears to be trying to be what he is not. He is failing in the attempt, as he must, and his failure is noticeable. And so he is not only a fool, but a buffoon. That is, a fool who has been caught. How many, though, never get caught trying to be what they are not? Granted they are more sophisticated than the buffoon, but are they any the less fools for their added sophistication? And of course it is not so much that they never get caught as that they get caught only by themselves. They are private rather than public buffoons. Shame has been avoided, but what about guilt? They try not to think about it, and they try very hard.

To look at oneself deeply, persistently, and honestly takes insight and courage. It is to attempt to see one's life as the expression of a set of values, and to isolate and evaluate those values. This may sound very simple; something perhaps for a Sunday afternoon. But if you think about it you'll realize that this kind of analysis is nothing other than an attempt to answer the questions "Who am I?" and "Am I someone of whom I can in the most fundamental sense be proud?" To answer these questions one must have some insight into what genuine human life is; what promises it holds in the optimum; what anxieties are fundamental to it; and what kinds of things are truly worthwhile. Courage is required because in applying these considerations to oneself what is at stake is one's entire sense of self-worth. Few questions are more threatening.

Although Kierkegaard emphasized the necessity of self-knowledge, of becoming transparent to oneself, his task must be distinguished from that of the professional psychologist and therapist. The middle years of the twentieth century could rightly be called the psychiatric age. The therapist, in all his varieties, has been the prime consultant for personal insight, either in his office or in his writings. In this capacity therapists have replaced clergymen, philosophers, grandparents, and friends. There can be no objection to some of the more restricted and well-defined practices and forms of advice which flow from the therapeutic community. Problems arise when much more is promised than can be delivered, and when distinctions vital to the practice of human living are blurred or unmade altogether. There are certain requirements, problems, and sources of anxiety which are built into what it means to be a person. To face these problems with courage, and to bear this anxiety with acceptance, is part of what it is to live a genuine human life. To characterize these human problems and describe these sources of anxiety is to philosophize. To assert and defend a view concerning what it means to live a genuine human life is to philosophize. When a therapist works to free a patient who is an airline pilot from the grip of acrophobia, there is little that is philosophical at issue. But when a therapist works with a person whose life is in point of fact empty and meaningless, to relieve that person of his sense of meaninglessness or feelings of guilt, there are philosophical issues involved. To confuse these two sorts of cases is to confuse the pathological with the philosophical. No matter what the therapist does in the latter sort of case, he must be working with some idea of what genuine human life is. This idea, this philosophical theory of his, must affect his practice. Even the claim that these two sorts of cases are essentially the same, and are both purely pathological, is an expression of a particular (and very common) philosophical theory.

Because therapists must philosophize, one cannot object *that* they do. But one remains free to criticize *how* they philosophize. They most often do it poorly, and by masking their philosophical assumptions in scientific, "value-free" garb.

Kierkegaard was a great psychologist in that he had remarkable insight into the complicated and often deceptive workings of the human person. But he also saw with perfect clarity what the limits to psychology are, and how the practice of psychology must ultimately be carried out within a more general commitment to some specific philosophical perspective. This would include a theory of human nature and a set of authentic human values. There *are* good therapists, but only because they happen to be, in addition to good psychologists, perceptive philosophers and compassionate human beings.

Kierkegaard's work, therefore, is not about psychology, although it is about the profoundest sense of "how to live your life." And although Ernest Becker was accurate in his ironic reference to Kierkegaard as a "post-Freudian," Kierkegaard was not primarily a psychologist.[1] To read Kierkegaard is to begin where you are now situated, with all those theories, assumptions, and values you cherish so dearly. It is then to be moved off that point to something deeper, more profound, and a great deal more interesting. It is to have your self rendered transparent to yourself, and perhaps transcended. It is in this sense that Kierkegaard is a philosopher of the human spirit.

I have written this book for the serious reader who is willing to put some effort into trying to come to grips with one of the world's finest thinkers. My hopes for the book are first that it will inspire you, my reader, to become Kierkegaard's reader; and second that it will give you the tools necessary to read Kierkegaard with reward. As you will see if you follow me just a little further, his authorship is very difficult to chart out. It is not possible, that is, to step in at some point, with some particular book of his, and understand what Kierkegaard has in mind. The "authorship," as it is called, is not merely a collection of books about different topics. It is a project in which each work has a part. What is necessary is a chart which provides some idea of the overall structure. With this, the individual works can be read with relative *intellectual* ease. But be reminded of my categorical claim that it is not possible to comprehend Kierkegaard as an intellectual exercise only. His entire body of work, with its elaborate "indirect" mode of communication, is constructed to prevent it. This claim does not, of course, extend to this little book. If you walk away from this book thinking that you now "understand Kierkegaard," my efforts will have failed.

My twin tasks of convincing you that there is something important in Kierkegaard's writings for you as an individual, and helping you to develop the tools to find it, are very closely related. For when you begin to understand what Kierkegaard is saying, you will understand that he is talking to you. The major task, then, is one of providing the tools for this beginning. The following are four principles which I have adopted in this effort.

First, no writer can be understood without some feeling

for his intellectual and conceptual milieu. You must have some idea of his problems, and of the options as he understood them. I am relatively dogmatic about this, and remain so even in our radically ahistorical times. When Kierkegaard asked himself "How should I live my life?" he saw around him two answers: "Live for yourself," and "Live for the good of others." The most sophisticated versions of each of these answers were represented by romanticism and by Hegelianism respectively. To understand Kierkegaard demands that you look, however briefly, at each of these views. If you are a reader with little interest in "historical perspective," read the discussion of these anyway. No one promises that Kierkegaard will come easily.

Second, since my point is not to present you with the "essence of Kierkegaard" but rather with the ability to read him, a certain amount of Kierkegaard's jargon is unavoidable. I introduce this slowly, and as painlessly as possible. If there is a long quotation from Kierkegaard which you are tempted to skip, resist the temptation.

Third, I have divided the book into sections dealing with theoretical contexts and with applications. This is analogous in, for example, Freud's writings to the difference between his so-called "metapsychological" writings and his case histories. The initial theoretical parts can be difficult and boring perhaps, but they are necessary in order to understand Kierkegaard's criticisms of the life-styles discussed in the latter part.

Finally I will say a word about style and mood. The issues to be discussed are of *fundamental personal* importance. Because they are of *personal* importance they do not lend themselves to detached, academic presentation. I have tried not to forget this, and to remember that there is a reader on the other side of the process. Where the urge to make an academic point is irresistible, I have exiled the point to the notes. Because the issues are of *fundamental* importance, I have kept the mood serious, attempting to avoid the frivolity both of pedantry and of cynicism. Thus the style is both informal and personal, and the mood is serious.

I.
CONTEXT

ONE

TO BE A REBEL

Think for a minute of what it would be like to have the remainder of your life laid out in front of you, in detail. What would be your reaction? At very least you would acquire a detached view of yourself, your life, and your future. Most likely you would strain to break the predicted pattern. In fact these two reactions are related. The detachment bred a view of yourself as "just one of them," the strain was to "be yourself." But each of us has had a view of our future, more or less. One feature peculiar to humans is the ability to detach ourselves from our lives and see ourselves as if we were "just one of them." For some of us the thought of this comes more often and stays longer. This type of person is described as "reflective," "self-conscious," "neurotic," "ironic," "pensive," "deep," etc. Not all these terms mean the same thing, of course, and they are used by different speakers with different attitudes toward the person who thinks a great deal about these matters.

As a young man Søren Kierkegaard was such a person. The time, let us say, was 1836. The place was Copenhagen, a relatively sophisticated city which was, culturally, a colony of Germany and always slightly behind the latest "trends." Kierkegaard at this time was twenty-three years old.[1] He was a brilliant, sharp-witted, extremely sensitive young man. His father had raised him in an atmosphere of stern, devout Lutheranism. His home had been a gathering place for the religious and civic leaders of the city, to discuss and argue about the great issues of the day—the political issues of a

11

postrevolutionary era, the social issues of an era of increasing liberalism, and of course the religious doctrines which permeated all issues. In these men Søren had seen his future, as a pastor, a bishop, a leader of the community. Now at age twenty-three this had been rejected. He would later have one of his characters express what he himself was feeling in 1836.

> Of all the ridiculous things it seems to me the most ridiculous is to be a busy man of affairs, prompt to meals and prompt to work. Hence when I see a fly settle down in a crucial moment on the nose of a businessman . . . then I laugh heartily. And who could not help laughing? What do they accomplish, these hustlers? Are they not like the housewife, when her house was on fire, who in her excitement saved the fire-tongs? What more do they save from the great fire of life? [E/O, I, p. 24]

But having rejected the bourgeois life of virtue, the life his father had planned for him, and his elder brother Peter had chosen for himself, where would he turn? To whom would he look for guidance, and in whom would he find kindred spirits? To someone of Kierkegaard's insatiable curiosity and voracious reading habits, this was not a difficult question. It led him directly and obviously to that group of young rebels known to later generations as "romantics." They, like him, had risen, in spirit at least, above the bourgeoisie. They had conquered the banal, overcome the predictability which was the straitjacket of bourgeois life. They had made their lives *interesting*.

In thinking about romanticism, the Anglo-American turns to the "Lake Poets," Wordsworth and Coleridge, but even more often to Lord Byron. Consider the young Kierkegaard in 1836 pondering the life and person of Byron, now dead for only a dozen years. Byron had been a traveler, a brilliant poet, a cripple, an outsider. His life was tormented by broken love, persistent malancholia, and by a terrible secret which he would neither forget nor reveal. And of course as all good men do, he died young in the service of a just cause.[2] About Byron you could say, "He really lived." His life had a depth and content which contrasted sharply with the tiresome and superficial repetition of bourgeois life. The *person* of Byron epitomized the young romantic rebel. Throughout Europe bright young men assumed Byronesque poses. We can be sure that the young Kierkegaard was no exception.

But there was a model of romantic rebellion which was a good deal closer to home. In the early 1830s a loosely knit group of German poet-journalists following the lead of the famous poet Heinrich Heine had become known as the Young Germany movement. Their names, Laube, Butskow, Buckner, Mundt, and Weinberg, are not prominent in the history of German letters. But at the time they were "the rage." Their work combined the genres of poetry and journalism, and continually agitated for liberal causes. They demanded democratic political reforms and an end to the political influence of religion. They advocated free love and the total and complete equality of the sexes in both law and custom. Their poetry expressed the themes of alienation and melancholy, the themes of a lost generation. The group was infamous enough to provoke the German Diet in 1835 to outlaw its writings, accusing it of being anti-Christian and claiming that it "wantonly treads all morality, modesty, and decency underfoot."[8] Of course the young Kierkegaard devoured everything he could learn about this group of rebels, and he thought about the "life-view" or basic philosophy which was at the foundation of what they were saying, and how they were living. He was never satisfied with arguing an issue for the sake of the contest. Nor could he discuss an issue in isolation from the more general philosophy which supported it. Kierkegaard was a deadly serious young man, always demanding to know what it would mean to *live* a particular view. How are they recommending that I *live?* Is that an *adequate life?* These were always Kierkegaard's questions, and as long as he kept these questions before him, he could never bandy about issues for the pleasure of it. Kierkegaard could never be a coffeehouse radical.

It was inevitable that even a brief investigation of the Young Germany movement would lead one to that group of poets and writers which was its inspiration and in every way its superior. I refer to the group of German romantics of the turn of the nineteenth century known simply as *Die Romantik.* Led by the younger Schlegel brother, Friedrich, the group included also August Schlegel, a critic and translator; the writers Novalis and Tieck; one of the century's premier theologians, Schleiermacher; and the brilliant poet Hölderlin. It included also two remarkable and, at the time, infamous women. Caroline Schlegel, August's wife, was thought by many to be the most brilliant member of the lot.[4] She would later create a scandal by leaving Schlegel for the famous young philosopher Schelling. The second was Dorothea Veit, the daughter of Moses Mendelssohn. Having left her husband, she lived openly with Friedrich Schlegel, who was to reveal the intimacies of their relationship in his novel *Lucinde*. At the outskirts of the group was the older Friedrich Schiller; and of course always there was the presence of the giant, Goethe, who could be placed in no class but his own.

As a group *Die Romantik* lasted for only five years, from 1796 to 1801.[5] But in that time it achieved lasting influence as a result of its reputation for outrageous behavior, its poetic productions, and especially its theories of criticism. But even more important, *Die Romantik* formulated a style of living which was to be the "model of rebellion" for the first half of the nineteenth century. It was an individualist, apolitical, "dropout" model of rebellion which would eventually be supplanted by the more political "left-wing Hegelians" led by such figures as Engels and the young Karl Marx. But it deeply influenced Kierkegaard and Hegel before him, both of whom after an initial attraction to it found it necessary to develop alternative life-views.

Perhaps the work of literature which represents most clearly the themes of German romanticism is Hölderlin's short novel *Hyperion* (1799).[6] Like Geothe's earlier and incredibly popular *Sorrows of Young Werther*, it is quasi-autobiographical, epistolary, and rhapsodic. And like all romantic literature it presents human life as a constant search for a vaguely defined state of peace and harmony, a state which in some form once existed but was lost.

For all romantics there was time in the life of the individual (childhood) and of the culture (Greece, the Middle Ages) when things were better, more innocent, more peaceful, less anxiety-prone. It was a time of harmony between persons, within persons, and between man and nature. But it was also a time when man's full *humanity* had not been developed, for the previous peace was derived from man's ignorance and from a lack of freedom. Man was still, in a way, an animal during this period for which the romantic felt so nostalgic. The break from this condition was in one sense a "fall," for its consequence was interminable dissatisfaction and anxiety. Yet in another way this fall was man's birth *as human*, for with it came knowledge and freedom. One could think of this in modern Freudian terms as the development of the ego out of the primary processes (the id), resulting on the one hand in a sense of self as separate from reality, and on the other hand in unceasing anxiety concerning the condition of this self. And just as Freud had difficulty describing how something so seemingly "non-natural" as a free person could emerge from a system which was purely natural, so also had the romantics felt this difficulty.

The change from natural to free being seemed to be a change which could neither be a purely natural event (nature could not create a non-natural being) nor a purely free action (a natural being could not choose to be non-natural). Rousseau had explained the fall as being an effect of a decadent culture, and the character of Werther had taken the same tack. But this merely pushes the question back to that of the origins of culture. Hölderlin has his character Hyperion state:

> But let no one tell me that fate parts us! It is we, we ourselves! We delight in flinging ourselves into the night of the unknown. . . . Ah! for man's wild heart no home is possible. . . .[7]

Man's fall to freedom and restlessness is somehow our own act and yet required by our "nature." The *human* heart is a free heart, but because of this, a heart where "no home is possible." Human life will have a complex spiral structure. Once the fall takes place, man is free and can never return as a human being to this previous state of ignorance and peace. Insanity and death were of course modes of return, but not *as human beings*. Despite this, there was a good deal of nostalgic and sentimental literature about these twin topics emanating from romantic quarters.[8]

Since a human return is impossible, man is doomed to search for a state analogous to his pre-fallen state, but one which includes the human characteristics of knowledge and freedom. In philosophic jargon, the onset of reflection and freedom has alienated a person from the state of immediate (unreflective) unity. In his alienated or estranged state man must strive to achieve a higher state of reflective (mediated) unity, thereby overcoming his alienation. But was a permanent state of "mediated harmony" possible? Most romantics thought not. Hyperion experiments with human learning but finds it irrelevant. He enters an intense friendship with Alabandra, but finds it impossible to sustain. He finds in the love of Diotima a temporary peace until she rightly points out to him that "there is a time for love . . . as there is a time to live in the happy cradle. But life itself drives us forth."[9] Life in this case was the revolution of Hyperion's fellow Greeks against the Turkish oppressor. He enters the battle. The expectation of action and conquest intoxicates him. His depression ends. His "spirit is firmer and swifter." His peasant army reveres and depends upon him, their gallant leader. And then,

> It is over, Diotima! Our men have plundered, murdered indiscriminately, even our brothers were killed, the innocent Greeks in Mistra. . . .[10]

But you should have guessed that it would happen. Recall that as Hölderlin writes, the French Revolution and its bloody and disappointing aftermath was fresh in everyone's mind. So the war was lost. Hyperion was exiled, disowned by his father; his Diotima had withered and died in his absence; he wanders to Germany ending his letters with the simple words "more soon."

Hyperion's life represented a human journey, a search. Every stage in Hyperion's journey was destroyed by his own naiveté. But each stage was "higher" and wiser than the previous one. The suffering encountered at the breakup of each stage was necessary to prepare for the next. Realizing this, Hyperion notes the crucial point, "He who steps upon his misery stands higher."[11]

Most of the central problems, themes, and images of romanticism are found in *Hyperion*: the idea of the fall with its ambivalent consequences, the spiral journey toward reintegration at a higher level, the experimentation with life forms, learning, love, national pride, action, friendship—the link between sentimental yearning and the mass hysteria of the Terror, and the romantic images of the person as wanderer, outlaw, prodigal child, rebel, lost lover, and victim of a consumptive death. All that was necessary to complete the picture of *Hyperion* as the perfect romantic work was for its author to die before the ink was dry. Hölderlin obliged in his fashion by drifting into insanity in 1806—never to return.

As the German romantic literature was developing, so

also were theories about that literature. In the poetic works new types of characters were created and analyzed with a view toward saying something about the condition of the new "modern" person. Yet the works themselves, their form, and the relation between the poet and the work were also thought to be new and distinctly "modern." This continuity between poet, poetic form, and poetic content produced works which were quasi-autobiographical. Often the writing of the work was the solution or therapy for the problems discussed in it.[12] Romantic criticism, by which I mean the theories of art of the romantics, went further to depict the poet as the exemplification of the new "modern" person. Friedrich Schlegel writes of the poets, that "they are the Brahmins, a higher cast, not ennobled by birth, however, but through deliberate self-initiation."[13] The term "poet" is meant here to designate "creative artist" and not just a writer of what we now term "poetry." As the ideal person the romantic artist replaced the gentleman scientist of the eighteenth century. Theories of criticism, of the poetic endeavor and poetic productions, replaced theories of scientific methodology as the focus of the philosophic concern with human nature. The poetic investigation of that form of depression called *Weltschmerz* (world weariness) became the question of the distinction between ancient and modern man. This question intermingled with the aesthetic issue of ancient (classic, naive) versus modern (romantic, sentimental) art. Both of these questions were analogous to distinguishing the child from the adult, nature from man. And so questions of aesthetics led to discussions of the fall, of the ideal life, of redemption from alienation. The idea was that a new era was dawning. All previous people related to modern man as the child to the adult, as nature to man. The romantics saw themselves at the vanguard of this qualitative leap. They were newly free, newly self-conscious, and newly creative. It was their destiny to develop not only new forms of poetry, but new *forms of living* as well.

This connection between aesthetic issues and issues in the philosophy of living was first made most clearly in Friedrich Schiller's influential essay "On Naive and Sentimental Poetry" (1795).[14] But it was Friedrich Schlegel who pushed the idea to its limits. The combination of his aesthetic theories, his scandalous relationship with Dorothea Veit, and his public depiction of the intimacies of that relationship in *Lucinde* sealed Schlegel's fame. He was the *bête noire* of orthodoxy, and the darling of disaffected intellectuals everywhere.

Prior to Schlegel's reading in 1796 of Schiller's essay he was a supporter of classic as opposed to (in his terms) "intéressante" poetry. He described the latter as subjective and stylistically anarchic, while the former, the classic, was objective and orderly. After his conversion to romanticism he maintained this distinction and simply embraced the other side. Emphasizing the point that modern man is free and non-natural, the stylistic anarchism of modern poetry is an expression of the difference between free man and bound nature. In form the poetry was to be as "unnatural" as possible, emphasizing the condition of modern man. The themes of the poems must likewise depict the truly human, which was the passionate assertion of heroic action and love. What follows then is Schlegel's famous definition of romantic poetry as a "sentimental theme in fantastic form." With the fantastic dominating the work, it is in Schlegel's term an "arabesque."[15] In the arabesque there is a seemingly arbitrary and chaotic mixing of forms and genres. The work is explicitly self-conscious and self-referential. It talks about itself, its author, its form, even the conditions of its publication. This all accomplishes an unnatural quality about the work. It is free. But how is it possible that such an unnatural being as the arabesque has been created? It is possible, says Schlegel, because of the fact that the poet is capable of the attitude of *irony*. Irony is the detachment, the removing of oneself, and thus the freedom which comes from being explicitly self-conscious, uncommitted and uninvolved in ordinary human purposes. The "ironist" stands back, watches, comments upon, and evaluates situations, never truly participating or getting involved himself. He then reproduces the situations in fantastic form in his imagination and in the arabesque. He romanticizes.

But to Schlegel and the other "aesthetes," the ironic posture was much more than an aristic technique. It was rather a *life posture*, an attitude of detached, superior, condescending scorn which came easily to a person (or a generation) which was socially disaffected to begin with. It is a posture of self-analytic, uncommitted observation of, and experimentation with, all possible elements of one's own life. The aesthete engages in "transcendental buffoonery . . . Internally:

the mood that surveys everything and rises infinitely above all limitations."[16] To assume this posture in life demands, says Schlegel, a complete lack of social entanglements; "even a friendly conversation which cannot be broken off at any moment, completely arbitrarily, has something intolerant about it."[17] In order to sustain the ironic stance one must be able to "tune himself . . . quite arbitrarily, just as one tunes an instrument, at any time and to any degree."[18] At the heart of romanticism is the rejection of orthodox social norms as oppressive and corrupting. The aesthete who assumes the ironic posture has conquered this society, not by altering it but by removing himself from any commitments to it.

Irony, then, is ultimately the romantic conception of freedom. This is not the freedom of the person who would "get things done," but rather the stoic freedom of withdrawing one's interest. It is an imaginative freedom. Having been frustrated in the "world of affairs" (Werther failed miserably as a diplomatic aide), usually because of his "honesty," the romantic accepts and in fact extols passivity in the face of this world. It is the power of imaginative reflection which provides for the "eternal agility" which is man's freedom, and the individuality which is to Schlegel the "eternal in man." The romantic believes in freedom and in individuality. He discovers both of these in the detached, condescending nonconformism of the ironic posture.

Friedrich Schlegel exhibited all these ideas in his famous (and for many years, infamous) work *Lucinde*. From a critical standpoint the book has been systematically and consistently panned. But as an illustration and statement of the aesthetic and philosophical principles of German romanticism, it was, and remains, extremely important. First published in 1799, it was republished in 1835 by Karl Gutzkow, the leader of Young Germany. It became the basic text for that movement. It was undoubtedly this later reissuing and the storm it created that prompted the young Søren Kierkegaard's interest in the book.

From a stylistic standpoint *Lucinde* exhibits Schlegel's idea of the arabesque, relating its tale in essays, dialogue, letters, etc. Its hero, Julius, is a man in search of himself. He writes an "Idyll of Idleness" in which he heaps scorn upon the action-oriented bourgeoisie as "those evil people who want to subtract sleep from life. . . . This empty, restless activity is nothing but Nordic barbarity" resulting in "boredom—our own and others."[19] Schlegel exhibits the theory of stoic passivity in a notorious passage, "a Dithyrambic Fantasy on the Loveliest Situation in the World." Here he makes the traditional male-active vs. female-passive distinction, and proceeds to extol the virtues of that "female" characteristic of passivity. He notes how Julius had played at being the female by adopting with Lucinde the female superior sexual position.

> We have to lessen and cool the consuming fire [of love] with playful good humor, and therefore the wittiest of all the shapes and situations. . . . One above all is wittiest and most beautiful: when we exchange roles and in childish high spirits compete to see who can mimic the other more convincingly, whether you are better at imitating the protective intensity of the man, or I the appealing devotion of the woman. . . . I can see here a wonderful, deeply meaningful allegory of the development of man and woman to full and complete humanity.[20]

Since life was meant to reproduce art, as ideally and romantically understood, Julius' life would mimic the structure of the arabesque which described it. Schlegel describes Julius' life as

> . . . a mass of unrelated fragments. Each fragment was single and complete, and whatever else stood next to it in reality and was joined to it was a matter of indifference to him. . . . he loathed the faintest taint of bourgeois morality, just as he loathed every sort of compulsion.[21]

Julius' search for himself ends with his love for Lucinde. The relationship between them was presented as totally fulfilling, and was taken by the German romantics of that and later generations to be the ideal of romantic love, and of human fulfillment.

Let's summarize at this point the discussion of German romanticism. I said that Kierkegaard, after rejecting for himself the future of solid, bourgeois virtue, looked to the romantics for an alternative. They had lived in a time of great changes, and were convinced that a radically new era was on the horizon. They were intent upon being at the vanguard of that era. Yet they did not choose politics as their vehicle.[22] It was social, cultural change which concerned them, and as revolutionaries they were social and cultural radicals. The romantic vehicle was art, rather than politics, and their issues were individuality, free love, woman's equality, the oppressiveness of social norms, the emptiness of bourgeois life. Their heroes were every sort of rebel and social outcast, but always rehabilitated, or as we would say, romanticized: the noble outlaw, the respectable prostitute, the insane, the cripple, Satan, the Wandering Jew, Don Juan, Robin Hood, the Prodigal Son, the consumptive woman, the frustrated lover, the noble savage, and of course the simple peasant. In place of the eighteenth-century emphasis upon rationality, they put passionate sentiment. The gentleman scientist was replaced by the inspired poet. The enlightenment ideal of social action was countered with romantic irony. The structure of neoclassicism was discarded for the arabesque formlessness.[28] The respectability of bourgeois marriage which in the ideal was neither a passionate nor an intellectual union was rejected for a "complete" relationship as depicted in *Lucinde*. The ideal of enlightenment optimism was replaced by romantic melancholy. The ideal of commitment to one's civic vocation was replaced by the extreme individualism of the imperative "Live poetically!"—that is, make a work of (romantic) art out of the elements of your life.

This then was the romanticism which Søren Kierkegaard devoured, not as an intellectual problem but rather to determine if it had in it a life to offer. Would a life lived romantically be a satisfactory life? This was his question. In answering it, he came to understand romanticism better, perhaps, than any commentator then or now. He understood it as it was meant to be understood, not as a style of art (only), but as a style of living. Eventually he came to his conclusion, and put the romantic alternative aside. His reasons for doing so will be examined later. These reasons are relevant not only to the ethos of the nineteenth century, but also to any system of values which emphasizes any form of narcissistic, dropout individualism. This would mean any system employing catch phrases (and catch ideas)—do your own thing, taking care of number one, tuning out, turning on, I'm OK–You're OK, building meaningful relationships, gurus, yogis, tripping, getting shrunk, total health, total sex, rolfing, jogging, tai chi, bioenergetics, etc. The point is not that any one of the above is evil, or harmful, *as part of a life*. But as a vehicle of your own human salvation, as the focus of your life, as that which keeps you going, any and all of them must be rejected as a gross insult to your self. Think of the proprietor of the world's greatest restaurant who literally "lives for" his daily meal in a fast-food restaurant. You would be incredulous. So much more should you be incredulous when you find a person who "lives for" any of the above. But this argument must wait until later.

TWO

THE DISCREET
CHARM OF THE
BOURGEOISIE

Y ou are, then, a person of some intelligence and sensitiv-
ity. You have in the past felt disinclined to become an
upright member of society. You felt in some vague way that
it would swallow you up, destroy you. There must be more
to life than becoming a cog in that gigantic mechanism. But
did you do that life justice? Were your criticisms fair?
Were they directed at what was *essential* to bourgeois life,
or did they fix only upon some of the more obvious perver-
sions of it? Is it in fact possible to live in society, committed
to bourgeois social ideals, and still maintain one's integrity?
To answer this question it is necessary first to know clearly
what the ideals of bourgeois life are, what it is that is essential to its system of value. Unless this is uncovered and subject to scrutiny, any critique of bourgeois life remains facile
and superficial.

I have noted that (although not yet *why*) the young
Kierkegaard rejected the standard model of rebellion, the
romantic hero. It became necessary then for him to examine
closely its alternative, that against which the life of rebellion
rebels. In so doing he was content with nothing but an investigation which went to the core. This meant investigating
bourgeois life at its finest. He did not have to look far for
concrete examples: his father, his father's friends, his teachers. Nor did he need look far for a comprehensive and
well-thought-out presentation of the theoretical foundation
of bourgeois life. He found the latter, so he thought, in none
other than the System, the philosophy of the German pro-

23

fessor G. W. F. Hegel (1770-1831).[1] Hegelianism ruled the intellectual life of Germany at this time. It had been introduced into Denmark by one of that country's most influential men, J. L. Heiberg, a poet, astronomer, philosopher, head of the Royal Theater in Copenhagen, and husband of Denmark's most beloved actress. It was espoused and taught in modified version by the noted theologian and later bishop H. L. Martensen. Kierkegaard was a friend of Heiberg's and a private student of Martensen's. He learned his Hegel well, but came to see Hegelianism as an articulate codification of bourgeois ideals, as well as a powerful defense of those ideals. It had, therefore, to be penetrated and destroyed.

This renders it necessary for a reader of Kierkegaard to have a rough idea at least of the general outline of this system and of some of its details. The following presentation is offered with trepidation prompted by the fact that Hegel's system is the most complex, wordy, outrageous, and inarticulate ever constructed. Despite this, Schopenhauer's comment that Hegel was "a flat-headed, insipid, nauseating, illiterate charlatan, who reached the pinnacle of audacity in scribbling together and dishing up the craziest mystifying nonsense" is most certainly false.[2] The System is remarkably bold in its design and often creative and brilliant in its detail. See for yourself.

When Hegel surveyed the sociopolitical-intellectual scene of late-eighteenth- and early-nineteenth-century Europe he saw it permeated by division, by opposing camps, contradictions as he called them. The people vs. the government; the theologian vs. the scientist; the needs of individual freedom vs. the needs of social order (witness the Terror of 1793-94); the young romantic emphasis upon passion vs. the Enlightenment emphasis on reason; body vs. mind; nature vs. man; inclination vs. duty; man as natural being vs. man as free being, etc. Some were theoretical problems (body vs. mind), some were practical problems (freedom vs. order), but there again is one of those divisions, theoretical vs. practical reason, reflecting a false distinction between thought and action.

Hegel believed as firmly as anyone could that these divisions, or contradictions, were only temporary and would resolve themselves at the proper time. The French Revolution did seem to teach that human freedom was inconsistent with social order; as soon as freedom was achieved the anarchy of the Terror ensued. But, thought Hegel, the proper sociopolitical arrangement could harmonize them. German romanticism in its irrational emphasis upon feeling did seem to show that one must reject reason in order to allow feeling its due, but the two could be made to coexist harmoniously. The French Revolution, Kant's moral philosophy, as well as the everyday experiences of marriage, parenthood, friendship, and vocation seemed to indicate that to do one's duty one must sacrifice some of what one wants for oneself. This conflict between duties and wants gives rise to two diametrically opposed ethical ideals, the strict duty-oriented view of Kant vs. the libertine feeling-oriented views of Schlegel and his friends. In practice one seems forced to decide between self-righteousness and perversion. Yet this conflict to Hegel was only temporary, and would be resolved.

These were not for Hegel purely logical difficulties. Europe was in turmoil. The promise of the French Revolution had faded. As Hegel sat at his desk in Jena completing his first and greatest work, Napoleon was victoriously entering the city. Serious thinkers everywhere were trying to discern the causes, and a way out. Hegel's view was not that these contradictions were unreal, but only that they were temporary and would resolve themselves.

Think of an analogy. When a child is first aware of its parents it views its parents as objects of need and love. The child in an unreflective way feels a unity with the parents, but sees the parents only as they relate to him, as *my* mother, *my* source of food, *my* comforter, etc. In Hegel's language it is a situation of *immediate unity*. As the adolescent begins to assert himself as an individual he rejects his parents as oppressors, old-fashioned, uptight, cruel, etc. Often the parents' own personal and family problems surface and exacerbate the situation. The immediate unity gives way naturally to a conscious, *reflective disunity* or alienation between parent and child (in the eyes of the child). Finally as the child works his way into adulthood he begins to view his parents as individuals in their own right, with lives, needs, problems of their own, and he accepts and loves them in full recognition of this. This is the final stage of *reflective unity*. This triad of immediate unity/reflective disunity/reflective unity is called the dialectic. The conflicts which concerned Hegel, and were mentioned above, existed at the stage of reflective disunity. The stages of reflective unity would resolve them. Hegel's system would lead men to understand this fact, and in so doing provide the way for that stage of higher harmony. Let's take a look, then, at that system.

As any great thinker does, Hegel invites us to look and think differently, from a perspective other than the one we would normally employ. He asks us to cast aside *common sense*. The universe, all that exists, is and always has been in constant change. That change is not just a rearrangement of matter in space, but rather is a development toward a very definite goal. The universe, then, has a built-in goal or plan, analogous to the built-in (genetic) plan which every human body has, determining its size, eye color, intelligence, left-handedness, etc. The human person is in no way non-natural but is rather an integral part of the universe. What people create, therefore, is in no way artificial, but merely the result of natural forces. And so the *theories* which the human species has produced to understand the universe are themselves part of this universe and so are subject to the same laws as those which "govern" the universe in general. Every significant part or aspect of the universe is a microcosm of the whole universe; thus the history of any significant aspect of the universe, natural history, art history, the history of religion, politics, philosophy, economics, etc., will show patterns which reflect and parallel the history of the universe as a whole. Likewise the history of the patterns of thought of a child as it becomes an adult will parallel the history of the patterns of thought of the human species in general. Thus the idea behind the statement "ontogeny (the history of the individual member) recapitulates phylogeny (the history of the group)" derives back at least to Hegel.[3]

If the universe is in a state of development, what is the goal of this process? And what is the structure of the developmental change? The goal of the process is for the universe to become a subject; that is, to become autonomous and self-knowing; that is, to become free. Think of a human fetus. It is almost purely vegetative, but through a process of development it becomes sentient, then conscious, then knowing, then self-knowing, and lastly aware of the fact that it is self-aware. At this last stage it is said to be autonomous, to have an ego, and, in the language of the nineteenth century, to have spirit.[4] But how can the universe, this vast expanse of matter in motion, be said to be self-knowing and autonomous? In the same way that a person, which is a system of matter in motion, can be said to be self-knowing and free. First the universe is mere inert matter, then it is (in part) alive, then sentient (that is, it produces from itself sentient forms of life), then conscious (that is, part of itself becomes conscious), then self-conscious (that is, part of itself begins to know it), then conscious of itself as not only the *object* of human knowledge, but also as that which knows itself, as the knowing subject. This last stage is the universe's consciousness of itself as a subject. So when the child's brain registers "that is my foot" we say the child is conscious of himself. When Isaac Newton said that between any two masses there is an attractive force directly related to the quantity of the masses and inversely related to the square of the distance between them, Hegel says that this is the universe knowing itself. The latter form of speech seems odd to us because we see Isaac Newton as an independent, complete being unto himself. But for Hegel only the universe, the Absolute, is this. Isaac Newton is like a cell in the brain of the universe. But Newton is unaware of this and so for him the universe is only an object of knowledge and not a knower. When Newton made his statement (1687), the universe was unaware of the fact that it is not only the object known, but also the knower. It is like a person examining a set of eyes in a mirror without knowing that the eyes doing the examining are the same as the eyes being examined. When the person says, "Those are my eyes," then the distinction between the examining eyes and the examined eyes is destroyed. So when someone develops systematically the idea that the universe is not only the object of knowing but the knowing subject (the knower) as well, then the universe will have reached the stage of knowledge of itself as Subject. This someone was, of course, Hegel. And so one claim of Hegel's system of philosophy was that his system of philosophy represented the universe's knowledge of itself, as Subject. His system represented the highest stage in the Absolute's self-knowledge. Along with this went the realization that the universe created itself, i.e., is a self-creating, self-explaining being. It is, in the language of medieval thought, *Causa Sui*. That is, it is God. And the greatest of its creations is its own self-knowledge as a subject, that is, Hegel's system.

If the above makes any sense, you may be tempted to suggest that Hegel is just talking about the same thing as common sense but in a different way. This is in a sense correct. He is asking us, as we said, to look at old things in new ways. But what goes along with this is not only that we will *speak* of things differently, but *evaluate* and *act* upon things differently. Let us ask, then, the second question: What is the structure of this development of the universe toward self-knowledge? The answer is, of course, the dialectical structure mentioned above. The universe is in the constant process of producing the opposite of any situation and then reconciling these in a "higher unity," as in our example of the child's attitude toward his parents. The opposition between immediate unity and reflective disunity is "mediated" in a higher unity, that is, the opposite poles are destroyed by being brought together and unified. This entire process is a *natural* one, exhibiting its own internal set of laws. It is also a *necessary* process. Each stage is a necessary prerequisite for the next and is "higher" or closer to the ideal than the one before. Thus just as the adolescent's cruel rejection of his parents is often *excused* with the quip "It's just a phase he's going through," so Hegel is often read as excusing human atrocities by placing them as phases in the Absolute's self-development.

We will now look at several applications of the above framework. These will serve as illustrations of the dialectic, as demonstrations of some of the consequences of adopting this Hegelian perspective, and finally as an introduction to some of the features of Hegelianism which is so rankled Søren Kierkegaard.

(1) Individuality vs. Social Obligation

We noted that one problem for Hegel was to "overcome" the opposition which seemed to exist between the romantic assertion of feeling and individuality vs. the Enlightenment assertion of reason and sociality. Insofar as to be social is to subject oneself to rules, this is also to discuss the opposition between conscience and abstract rules as the basis of morality. Hegel asks first: What is it about humans which makes morality possible? What, that is, does the *idea* of morality imply?[5] The idea of morality would make no sense without free choice, or will. Only if man has free will can he be held responsible and subject to moral laws. But free will is not abstract, it exercises itself in the manipulation of the external world, naturally giving rise to private property. Private property means possession, and the recognition of that possession by others. This aspect of recognition necessitates a contract of mutual recognition, and with this the idea of right (honoring the contract) and wrong (violating it) enters human affairs. Hegel is here claiming that private property is a natural and necessary consequence of the type of being a person is.[6]

> Property mediates the person with himself and with other persons. Although it remains external to the self, it is nevertheless acknowledged by himself and by others as belonging to a free person: he is respected when his property is respected. This respect is mutual and is the foundation for a legal community in which personal rights are secured.[7]

With the introduction of the idea of right and wrong, the questions must then be asked as to what is the basis for right and wrong. How is one to know if wrong has been done? Abstract rules (love your neighbor, promote the general welfare) are too vague. The temptation is then to fall back upon individual conscience. What is right (and wrong) is that which I *feel* good (or guilty) about. Morality is a *personal* matter. This is intended to preserve man's individuality, properly emphasize his subjectivity, and provide a way of distinguishing right and wrong. This view represents the moral doctrine of romanticism in its rejection of external prohibitions. But for Hegel, to rely upon personal conscience is to render evil as likely as good. In fact, Hegel goes further and identifies historic periods which glorify conscience with corruption, and claims a necessary connection between "Abstract Conscientiousness and Evil." More specifically, leave man to the dictates of conscience, and the result will be anarchy, evil, and perversion.[8] The only way out of this situation is to give content to moral principles not through general moral rules, nor through individual conscience, but through social custom. The Romantic Hero must surrender to bourgeois life (*Sittlichkeit*). The life of individuality must be given up for the life of concrete social duties, as friend, spouse, parent, professional, etc. In other words, a person who tries to figure out what is right or wrong using abstract, rational, moral principles will fail. These principles are too general to be able to be applied in actual life. The temptation then is to rely upon conscience, upon what *feels* right or wrong. But this, Hegel argues, will result in perverted sadism just as easily as pious altruism. The only way out is to identify right and wrong with prevailing social custom, bourgeois morality.

This, though, is not as bad as it seems. For societies change, and an investigation of the social reveals a dialectic. The initial stage of the social is the family. This is the stage of immediate unity. This "gives itself over to" the stage of civil society represented by the law-bound, spiritless era of Enlightenment capitalism. In this stage each individual has his own interest at heart. When these interests conflict, the law arbitrates. But "the atomistic outlook of the businessman loses sight of the ethical substance of the community, he understands the latter only in an analogy to his formal legal business contracts."[9] This is the stage of reflective disunity. The highest stage will be that of reflective unity, the State, where the wills of the individuals will coincide perfectly with the will of the Nation. Inclination and individuality will be synthesized with duty and sociability. This is the final stage, and most perfect stage where every man will willingly and gladly proclaim "my station and its duties." In this stage individual self-assertion is achieved through the acceptance of (resignation to) one's social place.

> The individual is grounded and gains his meaning through participation in the substantial life of the nation. Apart from this, the individual is accidental. . . . the general work and labor, which is the substantial life of a people, is particularized in professions, social institutions, and political differentiations (*Stande*: station, profession, condition of things, class, rank, estate of a realm). . . . To fulfill one's station in social life is doing one's duty, by which virtue or excellence is acquired.[10]

The point is that in Hegel's view he is not asking that we submit to bourgeois life with all its failings. Rather he is claiming that bourgeois society, which represents the alienated condition of reflective disunity, is about to change over to a higher stage which he called the State. To submit to the State is to lose one's bourgeois freedom, but gain a "higher" freedom. The influence of these ideas upon Marx in one direction and Hitler in the other is unmistakable.

(2) The Status of Christianity

Hegel arrives at his discussion of Christianity in the following way. He asks: What are the different ways by which man knows the universe? Or in Hegel's language, how does the Absolute represent itself to itself? The answer to this is called "the Philosophy of Absolute Spirit." The claim is that the Absolute can be "experienced" immediately in art; that is, that in aesthetic experience man achieves an immediate unity with the Absolute. Or the Absolute can be experienced as an *Other*; i.e., as something separate from man utilizing a pictorial or symbolic language in Religion. This is the stage of reflective disunity. Or finally the Absolute can be experienced as it is (and as it has been described above) in the nonpictorial, conceptual language of philosophy. This is the stage of reflective unity, and *is* Hegel's system. Thus philosophy subsumes and supersedes religion. Within the stage of Religion, Christianity is the highest form because it speaks most nearly like the language of philosophy (Hegel's system). And the "truth" of the doctrines of the state of innocence, the fall, the life of sin, the incarnation of God, the resurrection, etc., is exhibited by saying what they are "symbolically" referring to. For example, the incarnation, the central Christian doctrine that God became man, is shown to refer to the fact that the finite world is not essentially different from the Absolute. The idea that Jesus was divine and human is a pictorial way of saying that God and the world are one and the same. By having produced Christianity the Absolute becomes aware of this fact, albeit in a metaphorical fashion.

> This incarnation of the Divine Being, its having essentially and directly the shape of self-consciousness is the simple content of Absolute Religion. . . . this religion is the Divine Being's consciousness concerning itself that it is Spirit.[11]

Thus translated properly, meaning into the language of the system, Christianity exposes the truth. And Hegel never denied he was a Christian. But Hegel's philosophy supersedes religion by stating literally and systematically what religion hints at only pictorially.

(3) The Question of the Human
vs. the Natural Realm

With the rise of science in the seventeenth century, philosophers thought it necessary to conceive of the universe as a gigantic machine, as a mechanical system of inert matter. This produced the question of man's relation to this machine and forced philosophers to either (a) follow Hobbes and say that man is a natural being and thus a machine, or (b) follow Descartes and deny that man was a machine, and thus remove man from the realm of the natural. Hegel rejected both these views, by way of rejecting their common assumpion that nature is a machine. For Hegel, Nature = the Universe = the Absolute = a Self-knowing and Self-creating Being. Man then could maintain his qualities of self-knowledge and creativity and still be a completely *natural* being. The human realm is one aspect of the total universe, and no more need be said. The contradictory positions of Descartes and Hobbes have been overcome and absorbed into a higher unity which is the System. This system is able to comprehend in the same way, and on the same terms, Man, Nature, and God.

In summary of our examples, Hegelianism is able to point the way toward overcoming the apparent dichotomies between individuality and social responsibility, inclination and duty, religion and philosophy, man and nature. *In the last analysis* the central Hegelian vision is that Existence and all its aspects are purely harmonious, purely continuous, and purely one-dimensional. All conflict in the last analysis is unreal, and exists only because of an incomplete development. The massive effort of the System ends in an optimism expectantly awaiting universal peace and harmony in all aspects of life.

Kierkegaard saw this point very clearly. He also saw a relation between this belief in universal human progress, in the inevitability of a conflict-free existence, and the middle-class penchant for finding the path of least resistance, the middle-class search for the easy life, the easy money, the easy shared ideas, the easy Christianity. Thus when Kierkegaard erects an ideal man of bourgeois virtue (Judge

Willian of *Either/Or*, II) he presents him as a very intelligent and very perceptive Hegelian. More specifically, against the Hegelian view that all human relationships (parent/child, husband/wife, worker/boss, leader/follower) can be made harmonious, Kierkegaard argues that this can be done only by destroying the essence of the institutions (family, marriage, nation, etc.) which contain the relationships. To the view that the demands of social custom have an absolute validity, Kierkegaard argues that social custom can and often does present to a person corrupting temptations. To the view that rational philosophy is superior to religion in its presentation of the truth, Kierkegaard argues that philosophy and religion are two different realms which at times make contradictory demands upon the individual, forcing him to make agonizing choices. To the view that a person is a purely natural being, Kierkegaard argues that there is an unbridgeable chasm between the human and the nonhuman. In Kierkegaard's view, every one of Hegel's principles when applied in everyday life makes that life easier, but at the cost of a person's full humanity. Every one of Kierkegaard's principles, on the other hand, makes life more difficult, but with the reward of complete humanity. None of us is willing, *in the extreme*, to achieve an easy life at the cost of our humanity. We would not subject ourselves to lobotomies no matter what ease and peace it would bring into our lives. Yet Hegelianism when applied in social and individual life has the effect, Kierkegaard will argue, of a mass lobotomy. And the life of the lobotomized individual, the life which Hegelianism generates and legitimizes, is precisely bourgeois life. It is a life cluttered with compromises, where each time what is gained is a little bit of peace and what is lost is a little bit of integrity. Søren Kierkegaard was a person to whom compromise did not come easily.

THREE

TO COMMUNICATE
THE TRUTH

The time is October 1841. Think of Søren Kierkegaard on the train watching the German countryside pass by. The train's destination is Berlin, but Søren's thoughts are back in Copenhagen. He is in a terrible state. Feelings of regret, loss, expectation, relief, and terror compete for his attention. He tries, but is unable, to prevent his mind from rehashing, again and again, the last five years since his twenty-third birthday. His father's death in 1838 had been momentous. Søren had been certain that the old man would outlive him, and that he would have a chance to justify himself in his father's eyes. The death, which had left him an inheritance that would provide him a secure financial future, had jolted him out of his indecision; his future had now begun to take shape. Just this year Kierkegaard had completed his magister (we would say doctoral) degree in theology. His thesis had been a long rambling discussion entitled *The Concept of Irony*, which had received mixed reviews among his examiners.

But most of Kierkegaard's thoughts center around Regine. He had met Regine Olsen for the first time in 1837 while visiting friends. She was fourteen. Three years later she had consented to his request to marry him. The engagement was a social event in Copenhagen, bringing together two of its most prominent families. Suddenly Kierkegaard broke off the engagement and within days was on the train to Berlin. Too much has been written already about Regine, the engagement, Kierkegaard's reasons for breaking the engagement, his unconscious motivations, etc. I must say that I remain, despite it all, inclined toward the obvious. This is that Kierkegaard had decided upon a task for himself, for the remainder of his life; that he felt this task as his deepest obligation; that it contained in it no place for marriage, a family, or any of the normal domestic arrangements; that he canceled the engagement with Regine Olsen in order to get started on that task; and finally that he remained deeply in love with her until his death.[1] Clearly as an explanation, this is the romantic's choice; but Kierkegaard was himself a romantic person after a fashion. To say that he had a flair for the dramatic is to point to, but trivialize, the fact that he lived his life at an unbelievably high pitch, with a driving sense of mission. In dealing with this type of person the explanation which pleases the romantic often coincides with that which pleases the realist. Only the cynic remains unmoved.

What then was this task which Søren Kierkegaard had decided upon? The situation seems to have been something like this. As a young man Kierkegaard had rejected the future which we called the life of bourgeois virtue. He entered upon a serious analysis of the only other alternative which seemed to be available, a form of dropout individualism embodied in the thoughts of the German romantics. Having rejected this, he returned to a more serious analysis of bourgeois values, including his intellectual confrontation with Hegel, and his activites of finishing his degree work, and preparing for marriage. Yet this life was eventually rejected also. And what is more important, his rejection of each of these modes of living (later referred to somewhat misleadingly as "stages") was not a judgment of personal importance only. He rejected these "existence spheres" not only for himself, but for all others also. It was simply a fact, he decided, that neither mode of living was a satisfactory way of expressing the human spirit. The task which he set for himself was to *communicate* this fact.[2]

But how was this truth to be communicated? Should he finish his pastoral training and ascend the pulpit as a fire-and-brimstone orator? Should he enter the political arena to make speeches and promote reforms against the corruption of contemporary life? Should he write books condemning present-day life-styles?

No, an illusion can never be destroyed directly, and only by indirect means can it be radically removed. . . . That is, one must approach from behind the person who is under an illusion. [PV, p. 24]

It was not *theories* against which Kierkegaard was to do battle, it was *styles of living*, subjective truths which were also illusions. Thus only a "radical" attack was called for. The term "radical" here refers to the etymological meaning signifying "roots." The same Latin gives us "radish." A radical attack is an *attack at the roots*, and in this case at the roots of some prevailing styles of living. But this can never be done directly, because every style of living contains in it a way of dismissing or "explaining away" direct attacks. Think what would happen if you were to attempt to convince a paranoid schizophrenic that his beliefs were false by confronting him with evidence of their falseness, foolishness, and irrationality. One simple maneuver on his part and all your arguments are "explained away." You are part of the plot. His "theory" has absorbed *you*. Similarly the critic of the doctrinaire communist is unworthy of serious attention on account of his "bourgeois morality"; the critic of psychoanalytic insight on account of his "resistance"; the critic of Christianity on account of his "sin." The point is that any serious style of living has a technique for explaining away the critic by treating him as part of the problem. Thus a direct assault upon the paranoid's views will only land you at the center of the delusions you are intent upon destroying. Kierkegaard was aware of this treatment of the direct critic: "First and foremost, they do not bother about him at all. . . . the next step, they . . . settle themselves securely in their illusion: they make him a fanatic" [PV, p. 24].

Of course to reject a viewpoint on the grounds of some characteristic of its *proponent* is an error of logic, *argumentum ad hominem*. But it is often more than that; it is often a problem of courage as well. Our dearest values and judgments are elements of ourselves which we need very badly. To feel them challenged seriously is to experience something frightful. What is at stake when our style of living is challenged is a large part of our self-image, including our self-esteem; and this is a large part of ourself. It is no mystery then that if we sense such a challenge, we will respond with anxiety, and with our "explaining away" procedures. For such a challenge to work, therefore, it must be able to either *overcome* or to *avoid* these procedures. The techniques which certain religious groups use to "indoctrinate" initiates, as well as the techniques which parents use to "deprogram" such initiates, are direct assaults upon the "explaining away" procedures. These include starvation, sensory deprivation, fatigue, and intimidation, all standard prisoner-of-war experiences. Often they are successful in *overcoming* the defenses. To *avoid* the defenses is to challenge without being found out. It is, as Kierkegaard said, to approach from behind. If one is successful, the commitment to the style of living will be weakened sufficiently before the person notices it, and so the defensive procedures will be weak and ineffectual. How can this be done on a mass scale?

To solve this problem Kierkegaard looked to one of his few historical heroes, Socrates. In particular, he focused upon Socrates' attempt to communicate a similar message to the Athenians of the fifth century B.C. The method used then has since become known as Socratic irony. We have seen already what the romantics had intended by the idea of *living* ironically. To *speak* with irony is, in general, to be detached from your meanings, to intend something different from the meanings of the words employed. For example you enter a room in which there is a sumptuous spread of food. Your young child blurts out, "Wow, look at all that food." He does not speak ironically. You, however, do, when you casually note, "I see you've thrown together a little snack." It is ironic speech first because you have been explicitly conscious of the mode of communication, of your place in the situation, and of the fact that you stated the reverse of your true meaning while knowing that your true meaning would be understood. You are in a sense uncommitted to the impression or meaning your phrases would have. This self-conscious and uncommitted element is what F. Schlegel had found so attractive about irony, expanding as he did a mode of communication into a mode of living. For Schlegel the difference between the child's communication and yours would be a suitable metaphor to elucidate the distinction between nature/man, ancient/modern, and classic/romantic. Socrates had employed ironic (indirect) communication when he continually insisted that he knew nothing, had nothing to teach, and was a simple man who merely asked innocent questions.

Kierkegaard devoted his magister's dissertation to the topic of irony. He was extremely critical of Schlegel's ideas; however, he considered "mastered irony" to be an indispensable tool for evaluating one's life. Only by employing an ironic stance with respect to myself can I disentangle my consciousness from the everyday, from my values, my commitments, and my needs. Irony is the ability to "bracket" these and analyze my style of living from a detached, uncommitted, and thus objective standpoint.

> When irony has first been mastered it undertakes a movement directly opposed to that wherein it proclaimed its life as unmastered. Irony now limits, renders finite, defines, and thereby yields truth, actuality, and content; it chastens and punishes and thereby imparts stability, character, and consistency. . . . He who does not understand irony . . . lacks *eo ipso* what might be called the absolute beginning of the personal life. [CI, 339]

This is an important idea. Mastered irony is the insight and the courage to suspend or temporarily put aside your cherished commitments in order to objectively assess them *as if* they were not yours. To be unable to do this is either to be unable to step out of, and evaluate, yourself at all (fanatic, dogmatist) or to be unable to make any commitments worthy of evaluation (nihilist, unmastered irony). One must be able to be ironic *and* committed at the same time. This introduces a tension into (genuine) human living which cannot be avoided.

This point is worth expanding. What is the difference between a fanatic and a nihilist? The fanatic "believes in" something in a closed fashion. Fanaticism is not defined by *what* a person believes (a person can be a fanatical Republican), but by *how* he believes. The fanatic will not, or cannot, evaluate his own beliefs and those of his opponents objectively. He folds his arms, shuts his mind, and clings to his belief. For him the detachment of mastered irony is not possible. The nihilist "believes in" nothing, commits himself to nothing. For every answer, he can produce an equal and opposite answer, and he cannot decide between them. For the nihilist the commitment of mastered irony is not possible. Both fanaticism and nihilism are problems of courage. Mastered irony is the ability to be firmly committed to one's life while still seeing the other point of view.

Most men are subjective toward themselves and objective toward all others, frightfully objective sometimes—but the task is precisely to be objective toward oneself and subjective toward all others. [J&P, IV, 4542]

Mastered irony is then a technique that you must employ in your own life. It is also a technique you must employ if you are to communicate a *subjective* truth, that is, a truth which will change the way a person lives. The concept of irony had this twofold significance for Kierkegaard's task. First, it is an ironic posture which he will attempt to implant in his reader, as a first step. He will attempt to detach the reader from his own life long enough to allow him to see it objectively as a whole. Only then will Kierkegaard be in a position to suggest that it is unsatisfactory. Second, he will attempt to do this by means of communicating ironically with the reader. He will detach himself, Søren Kierkegaard, from his own words. He will speak the language, and express the ideas, of his reader. He will be more poetic than any Young German. He will be more Hegelian than any professor of philosophy. He will be more upright than any parson, more exploitive than any Don Juan. He will hold mirrors up to this reader, gradually broadening the images until what is reflected back is the particular reader's style of living viewed *as only one possibility*.

This will be accomplished primarily through an elaborate system of pseudonyms. The authors will at times have no names at all, referred to simply as "A" or "The Jutland Priest." At other times the names will be outlandish: Vigilius Haufniensis (the watchman of Copenhagen); Johannes de Silento (John of Silence); Johannes Climacus (John the Climber); Anti-Climacus; etc. Each author represents a perspective on a problem. Through the pseudonymous technique, the ideas can be laid out without the complicating element of their connection to an author. Simultaneously with the creation of the pseudonymous authorship, Kierkegaard was publishing books and discourses of direct communication. But these, he knew, were meant for very few, and primarily for those upon whom his indirect efforts had borne fruit.

It seems clear that as Søren Kierkegaard rode across the German countryside toward Berlin, his task and his battle plan were clearly fixed in his mind. He was about to enter upon a decade of intellectual productivity that few in history have come close to matching. Between 1841 and 1851 he was to write over thirty books. During this period also he would fill almost twenty volumes of private journal entries. All in an attempt to communicate his truth.

FOUR

WHAT IS A PERSON
AFTER ALL?

We are now in a position to get into the heart of Søren Kierkegaard's thought. In this and the next chapter I will describe in abstract terms (1) what Kierkegaard takes the human being to be most fundamentally *and* (2) the most fundamental ways in which the human being can fail as a person. These discussions will end the theoretical treatment, to be followed by Part II, in which the theory is put into practice in an analysis of styles of living. If you have stuck with me up to this point, there should be little question that you can finish. I realize that things so far, and for the next thirty-five or so pages, are rather abstract and academic. But they are also necessary. Recall that what we are after is a point of view which is both concrete (relevant) and profound (has depth). Such a point of view cannot be rattled off as a series of useful maxims, packaged in cute phrases and shiny dust jackets. It's this which we are trying to avoid. And more specifically, such a point of view cannot skirt the question of what in the last analysis it means to be a genuine human being, so let's get to it.

What is a person? The question initially stops you in your tracks. What are you going to do with it? Where are you going to begin? Some philosophers have said in frustration that the question should not be asked, that it has no meaning. But we can easily see that this is not so. A text in comparative anatomy has no difficulty answering the question with precision. Nor has the development of the law been seriously hampered by having to answer the question.

41

The answers in these respective areas will of course be different, but they will be relatively precise and uncontroversial.[1] This seems to be because the question "What is a person?" is in each case asked *within* a specific context which includes a well-defined set of problems, e.g., "How are humans physiologically different from dolphins?" or "How are humans legally different from corporations?" The problem with the question as we initially asked it was, then, that we did not specify what we wanted to *do* with the answer. So let's try it again.

We are interested in the question of whether either or both of the styles of living of the romantic rebel or the bourgeois person of virtue are adequate; and if not, what style of life *is* adequate. Adequate for what? For making money? Clearly this is not it; but if it were, the bourgeois life would be preferred. We mean adequate in a more fundamental sense, the sense of whether the person is living up to his fundamental obligations, is being all he can be as a human being, whether his life is or is not *being wasted*. Granted this is rather vague, but it cannot be otherwise because we are trying to ask the questions outside of any particular philosophical framework. The questions we are interested in can be described in the broadest sense of the term as *ethical*. To answer them we will need a relatively clear idea of a person's potentials for rational choices, for understanding options, for free choice, for adopting or not adopting styles of living, for working free of social and environmental forces, and so forth. To answer the question "What is a person?" only in the manner of an anatomy text is to leave these questions untouched and untouchable. So the question in our context is a request for a description of human existence, of the individual's *way of being*, which will be true, and which will lend itself to a solution to these broadly ethical issues. It must be an answer which is morally and philosophically relevant.

Thomas Hobbes (1588–1679) provided such a description. In his view a person is a purely mechanical being whose every action can be completely described and predicted, in principle, by the same laws which would explain the motions of a pendulum clock. A person is, then, a purely natural being, where nature is pictured as a giant mechanism understandable by the laws of (inertial) physics. In particular a person's behavior is motivated (pushed) by the interaction of his desires, where these interactions are pictured as vectors of motivating forces. This is a philosophically relevant view of the person. It has implications for questions concerning the nature and extent of free choice, of political freedom, of responsibility, of punishment, etc.[2]

Sigmund Freud (1856–1939) provided another such view in the twentieth century. According to Freud's view also, the individual is a composite of competing forces. But here the forces are arranged into three distinct systems, or kinds. There is a system of forces made up of innumerable demands for satisfaction, which are blind and unceasing. This system is called by Freud the id. It is the motivating element of the person. It makes him go. The second system also makes a series of demands. These are demands that the person be protected against the kind of cruel destruction which can happen if one is not careful and practical in the way he satisfies his instincts. This system developed out of the id as a result of the many times the id confronted the world and failed. It is called the ego. It has the ability to delay the id's demands (repression), but is fundamentally the servant of the id. Finally there is the system called the superego. It also makes demands. It requires that when you employ the ego to fulfill the demands of the id, you be careful not to violate those social rules and customs which others expect to be followed. The ego's demands are backed up by the anxiety a person feels when the ego is threatened. The superego's demands are backed up by its own form of anxiety, guilt. The superego grew out of the id–ego system, after the many times it confronted the disapproval of others (especially the parents). So the person is a composite of three systems of demands, the id, ego, and superego.

This is a philosophically relevant theory. It has implications for questions concerning the nature of human freedom, of actual guilt, of guilt feelings, of the most that can be expected of life, and so forth. I introduce this sketch of Freud's theory at this point not only as an illustration of a point, but because I will want to refer to it later to elucidate certain of Kierkegaard's views.[3]

Let's now turn to Kierkegaard's theory of man. This theory runs all through his writing but is presented most succinctly in one of his later works, The Sickness unto Death, published in 1849. There is at the beginning of that work a passage which has become famous (infamous perhaps) as a summary of Kierkegaard's theory. An exposition focusing upon this passage goes a long way toward explaining that theory.

> Man is spirit. But what is spirit? Spirit is the self. But what is the self? The self is a relation which relates itself to its own self, or it is that in the relation [which accounts for] that the relation relates itself to its own self: the self is not the relation but [consists in the fact] that the relation relates itself to its own self. Man is a synthesis of the infinite and the finite, of the temporal and eternal, of ∴ . . [possibility] and necessity, in short it is a synthesis. A synthesis is a relation between two factors. So regarded, man is not yet a self.
>
> In the relation between the two, the relation is the third term as negative unity, and the two relate themselves to the relation. . . . If on the contrary the relation relates itself to its own self, the relation is then a positive third term, and this is the self. [SUD, p. 146][4]

No doubt you will find this passage to be just so much "jargon." But in fact when you cut through its extremely Hegelian language to its meaning, it turns out to be amazingly clear. The (pseudonymous) author of *Sickness unto Death* is Anti-Climacus, who turns out to be a dry, humorless, severe moralist. He is a person who puts up with no nonsense, and his style is fashioned after that of his bitterest enemy, Hegel. It is also a style which befits its topic, which is despair, the sickness unto death. Let's begin, then, at the beginning.

Man is spirit. Note he does not say that man is *a* spirit. The point is rather that man is a spirit*ed* being. When you say, "I like a person with spirit," you are referring to someone who is self-possessed, who thinks for himself, controls his own life, refuses to be passive, refuses to be controlled from without. To say that man is spirit is to say that he is free, where "free" means not arbitrary or random, but self-controlled.

To say that the self is a synthesis is to say at the very least that it is a composite. It can be broken down into simpler elements. But there is more than one way for elements to be related. In the seventeenth century the French philosopher René Descartes (1596–1650) had said that the person is a composite of body and mind. But his view of the relation was that one was added to the other, in the way that breakfast is a composite of toast and coffee. To say that the self is a synthesis is to say that the elements which compose it are opposites, contrary tendencies, are (to use Hegel's language) in contradiction with each other. Think back to our hypothetical example of the Hegelian dialectic. The final stage of reflective unity between parent and child had two characteristics. First it was a state of harmony; and second, it developed naturally out of two opposing tendencies on the part of the child, that of personal independence (self-assertion) and union with the parents (relatedness). In Hegel's language these opposing tendencies had been "mediated" into a higher "synthesis." This had been a *natural* "transition" accomplished by the "negation" of the opposites into a higher stage (synthesis, moment) where the "contradiction" between self-assertion and relatedness had been "annulled." To Kierkegaard the self *is* a synthesis, a composite of contradictory tendencies. But he refuses to go the next two steps with Hegel's dialectic. The self is *not* a harmonious synthesis, and never can be. And the self did *not* develop naturally, but rather as the result of the effort of human will, "a positive third term." The difference between the two ideas of synthesis, and thus the two ideas of "dialectic," is the meaning of the distinction in our passage between seeing the self as a "negative unity" (Hegel's dialectic) or as a "positive unity" (Kierkegaard's). Kierkegaard will have nothing to do with Hegel's concepts of "mediation," "transition," and "negation."

> Negation, transition, mediation, are the three masked men of suspicious appearance, the secret agents (agentia), which provoke all movements. . . . In the sphere of historical freedom transition is a state. However, in order to understand this affirmation one must not forget that the new situation comes about by the leap. For if this is not kept in mind, transition acquires a quantitative preponderance over the elasticity of the leap. [CD, 73–76]

The idea here is that by using his technical terms Hegel leaves the impression that the dialectic processes he describes are *natural* processes, like the development of a rose from a seed, to use his example. But when you look closely you see that his stories make sense only because he has slipped in the idea of free human action under the guise of "mediation" and "negation." Thus they become "secret agents" in his explanation. Similar charges have been leveled at Freud, who seems to give a reasonable and naturalistic account of human behavior but only by turning the ego into a "little person." And it has been charged that Wilson's sociobiology seems to make sense only because he anthropomorphizes the communities of genes. In these cases the charge is that the attempt to explain human living without using the idea of a free agent fails because it slips in the free person as a "secret agent" disguised by technical language. If we were to reinterpret the hypothetical child-to-parent synthesis in Kierkegaardian terms, it would be seen rather as a tenuous and tension-ridden holding-together of the child's tendencies toward self-assertion and union. The holding-together would have been created by the child's spirit. This is the positive third term which Kierkegaard refers to. This spirit sustains the tenuous holding-together in the face of the temptation either toward self-assertion (rejection of parents) or union (rejection of self). To give in to either temptation would be cowardly, a case of weakness of will. The Kierkegaardian would, then, deny that these contradictory tendencies can ever be overcome and hold that the task is then to continually face up to the tension of the situation and to maintain *an* independence while engaging in community. The child-parent relation is only one form of social engagement. The problem can then be generalized from our example. Can there ever be a harmonious, tension-free compromise between my need for unique self-assertion and my need for human relatedness? The Kierkegaardian answers, "No." Your life includes the dialectically related tendencies. How to relate them properly is an *existential paradox*. It is a problem which human life contains necessarily, which causes anxiety necessarily, which each person must face necessarily, and for which there is no permanent "solution."

The idea of an existential paradox is crucial for understanding Kierkegaard. The discussion in Chapter Three pointed out the problem involved in the requirement of mastered irony. A person must be detached about his life, his values, and opposing values, while being at the same time committed to his own values. To be committed is to be subjective, to be detached is to be objective. A person must be both a subject (a center of commitment) and an object (an item of analysis) to himself. Yet these are opposing tendencies. They can never be made to live harmoniously together. They will always cause you trouble (anxiety) insofar as you attempt to satisfy both, and yet this is exactly what you must do. This is therefore a problem which is built into the requirements of being a person. That is what an existential paradox is, a problem (source of anxiety) which goes away only when you cease to be a complete person—in death, in insanity, in self-deception. A distinct existential problem exists with the opposing requirements of being oneself and being related to others, of self-assertion vs. relatedness. We have all experienced the threat of "engulfment" which too much relatedness creates. We fear becoming "nothing but" a spouse, mother, student, lawyer, etc. It is the anxiety of loss of self by being defined only as a role. On the other hand, to have no role is to experience oneself as a nobody, as empty. The existential problem here is to be an individual and be related to others. Neither of these problems will ever be "solved." They can only be "faced." To live one's life in the face of the demand to "hold together" the opposing tendencies within personal selfhood is to engage in the dialectic of selfhood.[5]

The self is constituted as a synthesis of opposing tendencies which remain always in opposition, but which are "held together" by spirit (will).

> While a genuine human being, as a synthesis of the finite and the infinite, finds his reality in holding these two factors together, infinitely interested in existence . . . [CUP, p. 268]

The human self is a break with the natural realm, the natural being the realm explainable by the physical sciences. It came about in a break with nature, and it is sustained by the constant imposition of the non-natural power of spirit (will). This means that human life involves constant effort, vigilance, and courage to maintain itself as distinctly human, that is, as genuinely or authentically human. The facts that anxiety exists, that human life is not easy, is painful, are not consequences of circumstances but of the very nature of human life itself. To have broken with nature (to be free) involves, as the necessary other side of the coin, tension, anxiety, constant effort. These can be annulled only by allowing the held-together synthesis to destroy itself. This would be an act of cowardice which would destroy the self as well.

Kierkegaard's antipathy toward the use of the Hegelian dialectic to understand the self was not, therefore, a matter of intellectual or theoretical curiosity. With these concepts human life became *in theory* too easy, oppositions *in theory* disappeared, all conflicts *in theory* were mediated. But *in practice* this could happen only to the extent that one rejected his status as a "genuine human being." Thus Hegelianism became a theoretical justification for the cowardly denial of one's true selfhood. This will be expanded upon later with specific examples. For now I would say that the so-called "human potential movement" that developed in the 1970s has as its (hidden) foundation ideas of mediated harmony very much like those of Hegel. And so the type of "salvation" which it promises would, in Kierkegaard's view, amount to a complete *loss of self*. This too must wait until later.

The discussion so far remains far too abstract, and will be so until the "dialectical pairs" or finite/infinite, necessary/possible, and temporal/eternal are explained. This will be done in a preliminary way now.

What does it mean to say that the self is a synthesis of the finite and infinite? These terms in philosophical contexts have always referred to the limited and unlimited, the bound and the boundless. Through the power of his imagination, a person has both the ability and the tendency to rise above his immediate circumstances to *imagine* a world radically different. There is in fact no precise limit to the way you can *imagine* the world to be. This imagination constitutes the "infinitizing" element in a person. Yet a person can also discern how the actual world *is* and how it *must be*. This is the "finitizing" element in the person. The two correspond very roughly to two of the functions of the id and the ego-superego respectively in Freud's theory. As people, we are expected to be both creative and realistic, both imaginative and down-to-earth. We are expected somehow to develop and yet check each of these opposing tendencies. Kierkegaard notes that the infinite/finite dialectic applies to our feelings, our knowledge, and our wills. To be a genuine person is to free up one's feelings (infinite) but in a way that they are appropriate to their object (finite). We must free our minds to see things in new ways (infinite) but in a manner which respects the "facts" (finite). We must free up our will to engage in tasks which change our world (infinite), but in a way that does not ignore the intermediate realities necessary to finish the task (finite). Imagination is the infinitizing element in a person, allowing him to break with the natural realm. But "reality" always remains, limiting the degree to which the natural realm can be transcended. This "dialectical pair" constitutes for man a constant series of "existential paradoxes," that is, situations which must be confronted but for which there can be *no precise rules* for successful confrontation.

It *is* appropriate, of course, to mourn the loss of a loved one, but not in a way that destroys your own life and the life of others (feelings). It *is* appropriate to envision a new physical theory that overturns Einstein's special relativity, but not in a way that ignores known evidence (knowledge). It *is* appropriate to decide to become a medical doctor even though you are now forty-two, but not in a way that ignores all the difficult steps that are required (will). Linguistically we smooth over the difficulties involved with words such as "appropriate," "realistic," "reasonable," "proportionate." But existentially, as existing persons, there are no clear rules. Only an act of our will can determine how it will be for us. Rules are impossible for the genuine person; life is too ambiguous. The struggle is perceptual, and so is anxiety.

The dialectical pair infinite/finite is the most general in Kierkegaard's scheme. The possibility/necessity pair is a specific application of that former dialectic to the questions "What shall I do with my life? Who can I be? Who can I not be?" I can conceive by the powers of my imagination many possible "me's": myself as great-grandfather, myself as good carpenter, myself as pope, as divorced, as president of the United States, as Emperor of Rome, as heavyweight champion, etc. All of these are possiblities *for the imagination*; some are also *real* possibilities. What determines to a large extent which are real and which are only imaginative possibilities is who and what I am now. Who I now am, the realm of necessity, interacts with the realm of (imaginative) possibility to create a set of real possibilities for me in the future. Without the ability to create a set of real *and* merely imaginative possibilities in thought, I could have no *human* future. But neither could I have a *human* future unless in the present I am a particular person. My future is determined by me as a working out of the relationship between possibility and necessity. This creates for me, as a person trying to create a future, a constant series of existential paradoxes. To live only in necessity is to live as if I am what I am and can be no different. To live only in possibility is to live as if I can be whatever I imagine. The problem is to hold together a synthesis of the pair. There is no way you can sit down, conceive of all your imaginatively possible futures, evaluate each one and decide which are real possibilities, and choose from that set. Nor is there a precise set of rules telling you, as you try to turn a possible future into an actual one, when to decide that the possible future is not a real possibility, and to give up. It all comes down in the last analysis to an act of the will; a leap, if not in the dark, at least at dusk.

To be blasé about the above is to forget two things. It is to forget that life's great tragedies are to be found in people who have cared too much (or too little), who have imagined too much (or too little), or who have willed too much (or too little) without having at the time a rule to guide them. Secondly it is to forget that *we often forget* that there is no rule to guide ourselves and others. And so in hindsight we are accused of foolishness, by ourselves and others. Who is the one who "would not face reality" but the person who had the same chances as the hero, but who failed where the hero succeeded? Rules are impossible for the genuine person, life is too ambiguous; and with this ambiguity resides anxiety.

The dialectical pair temporal/eternal is an even further narrowing down of the factors infinite/finite and possible/necessary. Every person must be aware of who and what he is now in order to determine who he can and cannot be. He must delimit imaginative possibility with necessity. To do that is to be free. When he does this, he is left with a set of *real* possibilities for his future self. So to the question "Who is it *possible* for me to be?" any of the members of this set of real possibilities is a correct answer. But there is a further question, which is "Which of these possible selves *should* I become? Which is the real me?" The idea here is that every person carries with him a real, true self, a self which he *should* be. This self is the "true me" now, and in the future, whether or not I accept it *as me*. The term "eternal" in the history of philosophy and in Kierkegaard's thought refers (minimally) to the unchanging. The temporal refers to what is *in time* and therefore changing. Our lives, surroundings, worlds, are *in time* and thus subject to constant flux. Who each of us is is constantly changing at one level. We grow, mature, marry, divorce, change occupation, have children or grandchildren. But throughout all this I am still I, and you are still you. And I am who I am even if I never became that person. The eternal element in me is both my continuity and my true self. It is the self not only that I can become but that I *should* become. The very worst thing that can happen to me as a person, my most basic form of failure, is that I do not become who I am. This is the general nature of all spiritual corruption, "for despair is precisely to have lost the eternal and oneself" [SUD p. 195].

And so Socrates' maxim "Know thyself" must be supplemented with the maxim "Be thyself." Socrates would not have thought so, since the Greek in him led him to believe that the latter would follow inexorably from the former. But as Kierkegaard knew, and as the Freudian phenomenon of resistance confirms, we have both the tendency and the skill to thwart self-knowledge; to avoid gaining it and to nullify it when it is forced on us. Whether we become or do not become ourselves is a matter not only of knowing but of willing. It is our responsibility and our most fundamental task. This then is what Kierkegaard meant by the expression "The self is a relation which relates itself to its own self." The existential paradox here is that while every person must change, respond to circumstances, not be "petrified" in the past, he must do this while remaining himself. And of course there is no formula for this. Life is too ambiguous.

In summary, then, the person is a non-natural being, distinct in kind from dogs or trees. It is his freedom, the ability to control his life (in part), which distinguishes man from the natural. This freedom presupposes his imaginative powers to conceive of the world as different from what it is, and to conceive of himself as different from how he is. This creates an *unavoidable tension* between who he is, who he thinks he is, who he could imaginatively be, who he could actually be, who he thinks he should be, who he actually should be. All of the problems involved in self-image, self-esteem, role playing, ego strength, ego damage, fear of failure, cognitive dissonance, etc. stem from these tensions. Ultimately they stem from the fact that man is a free being.

We live in an age which has been termed "the age of anxiety" and yet people still react to anxiety with alarm, with the feeling that it is something to be "cured." The concepts of the "dialectical pairs" and "existential paradox" suggest a different view. The surprising thing should be not that people feel anxiety but that they should be surprised when they do. Anxiety is a necessary part of genuine human life. It is the other side of the coin which contains freedom. As such it is an indicator of humanity. To be rid of anxiety is to be rid of yourself, that is, to be in despair. It follows then that all programs, movements, techniques, or belief systems which promise contentedness, continuous happiness, or anxiety-free existence are either fraudulent or demand that you pay with your self. That price is, of course, too high.

I would like to insert at this point one clarification about the idea of anxiety. So far we have been treating anxiety as if it were only of one kind. But think for a minute of the different *sources* of anxiety; threats to one's life, chemical imbalances such as low blood sugar levels, concern with the meaning of one's life, unresolved Oedipal wishes, agoraphobia, etc. Clearly life will involve some of these but not others. And the differences among them indicate that some clarifying distinctions ought to be drawn. I will use the term "existential anxiety" to refer to that kind of anxiety which is built into the nature of genuine human living. It arises out of the dialectical nature of the genuine human self, and as such is not susceptible to "cure" except by relinquishing one's status as a genuine person.[6] It can only be faced up to and endured, a life which demands courage. All other forms of anxiety I will refer to as pathological. Others, of course, have reason to distinguish between kinds of what I have called pathological anxiety, but I do not. This distinction between existential and pathological anxiety is crucial and yet is systematically overlooked by today's therapists. It is common to note that the types of complaints heard by therapists today differ radically from those which are so readily associated with Freud's practice. The hysterical paralyses and hand-washing obsessions were clearly emotional disturbances, and the concomitant anxieties were clearly pathological. There could be no *philosophic* objection to setting relief from this anxiety as the goal of the therapy. However, today's patients more frequently complain of disintegrating marriages, empty lives lacking in zest, feelings of meaninglessness, depression, hypochondria, and so forth.[7] In these kinds of cases the goal of therapy cannot be so easily identified. Should one attempt to relieve a person whose life *is* empty of his feelings of emptiness? Should one attempt to relieve of guilt feelings a person who is persistently unfaithful to a spouse? The distinction is crucial because the manner in which one should approach the problems is radically different. Pathological problems demand therapy to achieve a cure. Existential problems demand courage to reconstitute one's self. There are ways of helping another "take courage"; they were for example the stock and trade of religious pastoral counseling before the clergy lost sight of the distinction we are discussing. Existential problems are problems of the human spirit, and so long as they are treated as "merely emotional" the human spirit is denigrated.

Let's summarize briefly. The self should not be thought of as a relationship between two or more entities which just happen to have come to be related by some natural process, as water is a relation of oxygen and hydrogen. The self must rather be construed as a center of power (will, spirit) in which its elements are held together in spite of their natural tendency to break apart. "The relation is then a positive third term, and this is the self" [SUD, p. 146]. Kierkegaard's insistence and clarity on this point distinguishes his view from that of Freud. As Rollo May and others have pointed out, Freud's "structural" account divides up the self into three "agents" with no central control. That is, Freud has no concept of personal will. This theoretical defect is not, though, carried through by Freud in his practice as reported in case studies. There, the person is treated as a center of power, in control of his actions, even of those explainable only by unconscious intentions. It is worth noting also that some contemporary philosophers strongly insist that no sense can be made of human action without a concept of "personal causality" or "agent causality." It is this which Kierkegaard describes as the "positive third term" of the dialectic which is the human self.[8]

This preliminary analysis of what the self is can be further deepened by addressing the question of the genesis of the self. The question then is "How does the human self develop?" The manner in which Kierkegaard approached this question was deeply influenced by the romantic tradition. I have already noted that this tradition consistently portrayed the striving which underlies man's life as an attempt to reach a state of anxiety-free harmony analogous to his original state of ignorant naturalness. The most fundamental source of human disquietude for the romantic is the very characteristic that defines human existence *as human*, consciousness of oneself as separate from and in control of one's surroundings. I further noted that an attempt to explain the origins of this human capacity lead to a seeming paradox concerning how it is that a free being (a non-natural being) can derive from a purely natural being.

Kierkegaard attacks this problem most directly in his work *The Concept of Dread (Anxiety)*.[9] He noted that the paradox here was similar to one which theologians had faced in an attempt to explain "original" sin ("inherited" sin is a better word). In this case the problem was that if sin was not natural to man, then how could man have chosen it? Yet if it was natural to man, then how can man be responsible for it? Put in another way, you can "explain" the sin if it is a necessary part of human nature, but then it would not be sin; if it is truly sin it cannot be part of man's nature, and then it cannot be explained. Kierkegaard's interest in the quesion of original sin and its origins stems in part from the structural similarities between the questions of how sin first arises and how freedom first arises. But there is another reason that Kierkegaard discusses the origin of freedom within the context of the Genesis story, and that is that Kierkegaard agrees wih the idea that the life of every person involves a spiritual corruption (despair) for which the person is responsible. He further believes that this corruption originates simultaneously with the origins of freedom. The concept of despair will be developed in the next chapter; for now we will concentrate upon the origins of freedom, and thus of self.[10]

In the beginning, says Kierkegaard, each person exists in a state of harmony within himself, and with his environment. This is a state in which man is "soulishly determined in immediate unity with his natural condition" [CD, 37]. It is a state of ignorance and of innocence. Being in unity with his natural condition, the person is yet only potentially human, "spirit is dreaming in man." This is the condition allegorically described in the myth of the Garden of Eden. But something disturbs this state. From outside of Adam, a prohibition is introduced.

> The prohibition alarms Adam [induces in him a
> state of dread] because the prohibition awakens in
> him the possibility of freedom. That which passed
> innocence by as the nothing of dread has now en-
> tered him, and here again it is a nothing, the alarm-
> ing possibility of *being able*. What he is able to do,
> of that he has no conception. . . . [CD, p. 40]

What is it then which shakes a person free of his natural
condition of ignorant harmony? Initially it is a prohibition
of some kind. When this prohibition is understood, when
the person understands the "you-may-not," that entails that
he has understood the "I can." But this is to have a conception of one's ability to control one's self. It is to understand
the *possibility* of one's own freedom. It is not yet to *be* free.
Kierkegaard is not giving here a step-by-step account of the
origin of the concept of self and thus of the self. He is
rather stating some of the necessary elements for such a
concept, the most important being a sense of the self's ability
to control itself. He is pointing out also that this arises in a
social context of norms and regulations.

It may be instructive at this point to take a look at
Freud telling the same story.

> . . . the state of mental equilibrium was originally
> disturbed by the peremptory demands of inner
> needs. . . . Whatever was thought of was simply
> imagined in an hallucinatory form. . . . This at-
> tempt at satisfaction by means of hallucination was
> abandoned . . . because of the disappointment ex-
> perienced. Instead the mental apparatus had to de-
> cide to form a conception of the real circumstances
> in the outer world and to exert itself to alter
> them. . . .[11]

Like Kierkegaard, Freud is also not giving a step-by-step description of the development of the self (ego). His anthro-
pomorphic language clearly indicates this. But he does see
the development as the result of a collision between the
early harmonious state and an intractable external force.
And he does see the crucial difference in the development to
be the existence of knowledge ("a conception of the real")
and freedom ("to exert itself to alter them").[12]

What then is the response of the self to its new understanding of its own powers, to its freedom? To Kierkegaard, the response is one of perfectly symmetrical

ambivalence. Something is ambivalent if it is experienced as both desirable and undesirable. The self experiences its own power as at the same time *attractive* and *repulsive, desirable* and *fearsome.* Think of your reaction upon happening onto a terrible auto accident. You stare, strain your neck to see, and yet you don't want to look, you want to get away. Kierkegaard names this ambivalence "dread," and to emphasize its symmetry he defines it as "sympathetic antipathy and antipathetic sympathy" [CD, p. 38].

> In dread there is the egoistic infinity of possibility, which does not tempt like a definite choice, but alarms [*angster*] and fascinates with its sweet anxiety [*beangstelse.*] [CD, p. 55]

Everything up to this point is fully natural and explainable psychologically. It has followed the natural progression: state of immediate unity—prohibition—awareness of the possibility of freedom—the ambivalence of dread. At this point the unexplainable happens. What occurs is on the one hand a person's first act of freedom and on the other hand his first attempt to be something different from what he really is (despair).

> Thus dread is the dizziness of freedom which occurs when the spirit would posit the synthesis, and freedom then gazes down into its own possibility, grasping at finiteness to sustain itself. In this dizziness freedom succumbs. Further than this psychology cannot go and will not. That very instant everything is changed, and when freedom rises again it sees that it is guilty. Between these two instants lies the leap, which no science has explained or can explain. [CD, p. 55]

Every person's attitude toward his own freedom is one of ambivalence. Every person when confronted with his own freedom attempts to draw back from it, to "grasp at finiteness." Why does a person do this? There can be no naturalistic explanation. Insofar as psychology is a natural science, it can take you up to the dread but no further. There occurs in the face of dread a leap; on the other side is *human* existence. This type of existence is understood and explained in a different, non-natural way.

Kierkegaard recognizes that some people may be put off

by his appropriation of the Genesis story to make his points. His answer is that we should try

> ... reminding ourselves that no age has been more intent upon producing myths as our own, which is producing myths at the same time that it wants to extirpate all myths. [CD, p. 42]

He is also aware of the fact that some will demand an "explanation" of what he calls the "leap." But this demand "is a stupidity which could only occur to people who are comically anxious to get an explanation" [CD, p. 45]. The fact simply is that existence in general is not in its entirety subject to the same kinds of understanding, or the same kinds of laws. Between the human realm and the natural realm there is a chasm which is traversed when the dreaming spirit first exercises freedom. From that point on natural science remains relevant, but its perspective upon human life must be partial. Human life must be "understood" not only in naturalistic terms but in terms of moral concepts of responsibilities, rights, obligations, and guilt (actual guilt, not only legal guilt or guilt "feelings"). Any attempt to try to absorb the later concepts into a scientific perspective (psychology, sociology, anthropology, law, etc.) would be to destroy them, and the human person with them.

The ordinary reader will wonder, perhaps, why this needs statement at all, and more generally why I keep harping on this point about the difference *in kind* between the human and the natural realm. And of course this reader is correct; it should not need emphasis. But alas it does. For if there are social scientists (or any believers in social science) who have followed me up to here, you will know that a good deal of the social science in the twentieth century has been an attempt to absorb the human into the natural. Perhaps someday there will be a conception of the natural which will render this absorption reasonable, but I suspect that if this occurs it will be after the conception of the natural has first been absorbed into that of the personal.

Let us now summarize Kierkegaard's conception of the self, that is, of the person, in a way that will bring out the philosophically relevant and interesting aspects of his theory.

To answer the question "What is a person?" is to give a description of human existence which is relevant to some specific set of problems. Kierkegaard is interested in what it means to be a *genuine* person, a person who is all he can be. He defines the self as a synthesis, but declines Hegel's tactic of describing all syntheses as naturally developed harmonies of previously opposing elements. The self is a synthesis of elements which are and will always remain in opposition. These elements are "held together" by the person and involve a tension or an anxiety which is a constant temptation to the person to "let it go." This would be a cowardly act, destroying the self in order to escape the anxiety. The forms of "letting go" are the forms of despair and will be discussed shortly. The constituted self is in control of itself and thus is free. Its reaction to its own freedom is one of attraction (thus the "holding together") and repulsion (thus the "letting go"). This reaction is called dread. Because the self is free, it must be understood by supplementing naturalistic modes of thought with moral and philosophical concepts. Finally this all entails that anxiety and genuine humanness are inextricably bound together. Far from being something to be avoided or cured, (existential) anxiety is the indicator of genuine, morally acceptable living. But as a matter of fact, every person to some extent, using some device, attempts to alleviate his own anxiety by relinquishing somewhat his genuine humanness. This is despair, and is our next topic.

FIVE

A THEORY OF
HUMAN CORRUPTION

Every theory which pretends to say something significant about human life includes not only an idea about how human life could *best* be lived, but also an idea about the ways in which human life goes wrong. These we could call in general the forms of human corruption. These theories will also include some account of the origins or causes of that corruption. Thus Freud describes the forms of neurosis and their origins in the psychosexual development of the individual. Marx describes the forms of human alienation and their origins in the economic structure, the mode of production, of society. So also Kierkegaard describes the forms of despair and their origins in the self-deceptive acts of the person. The idea here is that each kind of being can "go wrong" or experience corruption in its own particular way. If people were purely physical beings in the sense that the language of the physical sciences was completely adequate to understand them, then human corruption would equal physical disease. If people were purely psychological beings (angels, perhaps), then human corruption would equal madness. If people were purely social beings, then human corruption would equal ostracism, and so forth. The theory of corruption which any social thinker promotes will depend upon what he thinks a person is, most fundamentally. Thus neurosis (Freud), alienation (Marx), and despair (Kierkegaard) are all terms denoting the specifically and uniquely human forms of corruption. On the other hand, what these terms describe are very different, because each of

59

these thinkers has a different idea of what a person is, most fundamentally.

We have by now a good idea of how Kierkegaard thinks of the human person, of his nature, and of the existential, that is, unavoidable, problems of his life. We saw that dread is the ambivalent response of every person to the initial possibility of freedom, and that dread is the continued response to the problems of holding together the dialectic which is the self. When a person "lets go," and fails to hold the self together, then its elements assume an improper relationship. The person may find that this soothes his dread, but it does so at too high a cost. From the disinterested standpoint of psychology this is despair, "a disrelationship in a relation which relates itself to itself" [SUD, p. 147]. From a moral standpoint, despair is sin. Although it is appropriate to investigate despair psychologically, it must be warned that despair is a sickness of *spirit* and that if one sees psychological problems on an analogy to medical problems then the nature of despair will be missed. It is in *The Sickness unto Death* that Kierkegaard discusses despair most completely.

It should be clear from the start that despair is not a feeling, an attitude, an emotion, or any other cognitive or effective state. To be in despair is not the same as to be "without hope" as the etymology of the word would indicate. Nor is it necessarily to be "depressed." Despair is a condition of the human self, whether it is felt or known or whether it is completely out of consciousness. It is a disrelationship in the dialectical structure of the self. Freud's thought contains (implicitly) two concepts of anxiety: anxiety as a feeling which signals a danger to the ego (signal anxiety), and "structural anxiety" which is the actual condition of ego disintegration. These two concepts correspond in Kierkegaard to the concepts of dread and despair, respectively.[1] The point must be stressed that there is no unique feeling associated with despair. As a structural disrelationship one can compare it, as Kierkegaard does, to tuberculosis. The latter is a structural-physiological condition that may be felt as depression, elation, fatigue, contentment, or not at all (in the beginning). There is no "feeling of tuberculosis." So for Kierkegaard there is no "feeling of despair," although if and when it progresses despair will produce all sorts of different feelings.

Thinking back to our discussion of romanticism we recall that "the fall" was an ambivalent event in the life of the individual. It creates restlessness and tension and yet freedom and knowledge.

> Is despair an advantage or a drawback? Regarded in a purely dialectical way it is both. . . . The possibility of this sickness is man's advantage over the beast. . . . So then it is an infinite advantage to be able to despair; and yet, it is not only the greatest misfortune and misery to be in despair; no it is perdition. [SUD, p. 148]

To be able to despair is at the same time to be able to have a self.[2] To be in despair is to be sick in one's most precious quality because "to have a self, to be a self, is the greatest concession made to man, but at the same time it is eternity's demand upon him" [SUD, p. 154]. To be in despair is to choose to fail that demand.

The concept of despair as a structural disrelationship of the self can be made more specific by considering in a very broad fashion its types. Since despair is a disrelationship in the dialectical elements of the self, one way to classify its types is to think of the ways these elements can be disrupted. Think for a minute of Freud's structural description of the self as the system of id, ego, and superego. This would lead to a classification of "disorders" such as: (1) impulsive to psychotic (id emphasis), (2) pragmatic to psychopathic (ego emphasis), (3) self-righteous to guilt-obsessive (superego emphasis). To think in this way is to ignore for a time the question of the origins of the disorders and thus of the part played by the conscious, preconscious, and unconscious. So also Kierkegaard titles section III, A of *The Sickness unto Death*, "Despair regarded in such a way that one does not reflect whether it is conscious or not, so that one reflects only upon the factors of the synthesis" [SUD, p. 162]. Looked at this way, there can be two forms of despair under each of the pairs finitude/infinitude, possibility/necessity.

With regard to the former pair one can lack a sufficient degree of finitude (the despair of infinitude). What would this mean? Kierkegaard adopts the traditional division of man's conscious life into feeling, thinking, and willing. To lack finitude is to *feel* things to a degree which is out of proportion to their objective importance—for example, the person we call hypersensitive. In the extreme the *object* of feeling loses importance and it is the feeling itself which be-

comes important, "becoming a sort of abstract sentimental-
ity" [SUD, p. 164]. One can think of a couple who takes
their "relationship" very seriously, constantly discussing and
analyzing it, *and* how each feels about it. The (incorrect)
assumption that a relationship is healthy to the degree that
each has "good feelings" about it can become so embedded
that the relationship ceases to be a topic of discussion, leaving only the "feelings" of each about it to be analyzed. Once
this happens the relationship is likely to be terminally ill.
Similarly, to lack finitude is to *think* of matters far removed
from real concerns, from evidence, or from relevance. Man
develops "a kind of inhuman knowing for the production of
which man's self is squandered" [SUD, p. 164]. Finally man
begins to *will* the impossible, that is, to will to achieve a goal
without regard for the practical steps necessary to accomplish it.

> And when feeling, or knowledge, or will have thus
> become fantastic, the entire self may at last become
> so. . . . The self thus leads a fantastic existence in
> abstract endeavor after infinity, or in abstract isola-
> tion, constantly lacking itself, from which it merely
> gets further and further away. . . . But in spite of
> the fact that a man has become fantastic in this fash-
> ion, he may nevertheless (although most commonly
> it becomes manifest) be perfectly well able to live
> on, to be a man, as it seems, to occupy himself with
> temporal things, get married, beget children, win
> honor and esteem and perhaps no one notices that in
> a deeper sense he lacks a self. [SUD, p. 165]

Ernest Becker finds in this description a rich and perceptive
description of psychosis, including those whom we would
perhaps call the "ambulatory schizophrenics."[3] It is surely
this, but it is also a description of a certain sort of "normal"
pathology. Kierkegaard was not interested in drawing lines
between sanity and madness. He preferred to see it more as
a continuum, much in the way of those today who stress the
continuity between cognitive styles and neurotic styles.[4]
Within the "normal" realm it is easy to see that it was the
romantic existence which Kierkegaard characterizes as the
despair of infinitude, with the example of F. Schlegel ever in
mind.

The other half of the first pair is the despair which lacks

infinitude (the despair of finitude). This is the self which is lost,

> . . . not by evaporation in the infinite, but by being entirely finitized, by having become, instead of a self, a number, just one man more, one more repetition . . . and while it is true that every self as such is angular, the logical consequence of this merely is that it has to be polished, not that it has to be ground smooth. [SUD, p. 166]

This person permits himself "as it were to be defrauded by others." He throws himself into the world, becomes wise about its ways, and forgets his own name. He finds "it too venturesome a thing to be himself, far easier to be an imitation, a number, a cipher in the crowd." He sees to it that he is "ground smooth as a pebble, courant as a well-used coin" [SUD, p. 167].

Thus one can reject himself by living in abstraction, fleeing from the world; or one can reject himself by becoming the crowd, fleeing into the world. The former corresponds to the romantic life, the latter to the bourgeois. *Human* existence includes the capacity to separate oneself consciously from all else, but also the requirement that contact be maintained with the other. This constitutes an existential problem, and a challenge, the challenge to be an individual while living in the concrete. The point is to be a *concrete individual,* which is the proper synthesis of finitude and infinitude.

The second dialectical pair is that of possibility/necessity. Here one can lack necessity (the despair of possibility). Apply the despair of infinitude to the question "Who shall I become?" and the result is the despair of possibility. Without analyzing who and what I now am, I dream of all the imaginatively possible future "me's," but I do not "budge from the spot, nor get to any spot, for precisely the necessary is the spot; to become oneself is precisely a movement at the spot" [SUD, p. 167]. At the extreme this is the person who each day rethinks his future.

> At the instant something appears possible, and then a new possibility makes its appearance, at last this phantasmagora moves so rapidly that it is as if everything were possible and this is precisely the last moment, when the individual becomes for himself a

> mirage. . . . What really is lacking the power to
> obey, to submit to the necessity in oneself. . . .
> [SUD, p. 167]

To see myself in a mirror I must first know my own face,
otherwise it would be merely another person staring at me
from the mirror. So to see myself truly reflected in the future of possibility I must know who I am now.

Finally one can despair by lacking possibility (the
despair of necessity). Again, applying the despair of finitude
to the question "Who shall I become?" generates the despair
of necessity. This person has fled into the world because he
found life too venturesome. If the question "Who shall I become?" is forced upon him, he answers with a line from the
fatalist, "I will be who I am, which is what I must be." His
strategy is to give up hope ("everything has become necessary") or to give up desire ("everything has become
trivial"). In either case he has rationalized his lack of "movement at the spot."

To be a *free being* is to be in control of one's own life,
of deciding who one will be. I relinquish that freedom when
I revel in the dream world of possibility and never "move
from the spot," or when I submit to the everyday and never
"move from the spot." The proper synthesis of possibility
and necessity is freedom.

While it is perfectly correct to categorize forms of
despair in the ways just described, it is not the most significant classification.

> Principally . . . despair must be viewed under the
> category of consciousness: the question whether
> despair is conscious or not, determines the qualita-
> tive difference between despair and despair. In its
> concept all despair is doubtless conscious; but from
> this it does not follow that he in whom it exists . . .
> is himself conscious of it. It is in this sense that con-
> sciousness is decisive. [SUD, p. 162]

Socrates had said that knowledge leads inevitably to virtue, that no man would knowingly do evil. This odd idea
resulted from his beliefs first that to do evil is to harm
oneself and second that no man would knowingly harm himself. Thus evil results from ignorance, it is a mistake. But
this will not do. A genuine mistake is something for which
we are not responsible, and thus it could not be evil. To

equate evil with ignorance or with any other form of inability is to deny evil. Socrates' mistake is repeated today by those who treat evil actions and evil people with social/medical labels of "deviance," "maladjustment," etc. If mugging and raping old people is a consequence of an inability to adjust to social norms, then it is no more evil than an earthquake. The Judeo-Christian tradition developed a different idea about evil. It was *a requirement* of an evil act that it be done intentionally, that is, with knowledge. Yet how, Socrates would ask, can you believe that a person would intentionally do something so damaging to himself? And within the Judeo-Christian tradition, to do evil is certainly to do damage to oneself. And so there is a paradox, or so it seems. If evil action is truly damaging to oneself, one would never knowingly do it; yet if one does evil out of the inability of ignorance it is not really evil. To hold that evil is self-damaging and is done knowingly seems to be inconsistent.

Kierkegaard gets himself into this seemingly inconsistent position when he claims that despair is a "sickness unto death" for the individual, *and yet,*

> ... at every actual instant of despair the despairer bears as his responsibility all the foregoing experience in possibility as a present. This comes from the fact that despair is a qualification of spirit. [SUD, p. 150]

Despair is a sickness which is freely chosen and for which the person is continually responsible. The motive for despair is the cowardly attempt to escape the anxiety of genuine selfhood. But how is it possible that one could knowingly choose to be sick? Socrates' question still makes sense. Kierkegaard's answer to the question lies in the capacity of a person to create and maintain "a half obscurity about his own condition."

> At one moment it has almost become clear to him that he is in despair; but then at another moment it appears to him after all as though his indisposition might have another ground ... something outside of himself, and if this were to be changed, he would not be in despair. Or perhaps, by diversions, or in other ways, e.g., by work and busy occupations as means of distraction, he seeks by his own effort to preserve an obscurity about his condition ... or

> perhaps he is even conscious that he labors thus in
> order to sink the soul into obscurity. . . . For in
> fact there is in all obscurity a dialectical interplay of
> knowledge and will. . . . [SUD, p. 181]

This is an absolutely crucial passage in Kierkegaard's theory
of human corruption. It describes the foundations of a theory of self-corruption in which there is no paradox involved
in the idea that a person will knowingly (responsibly) cor-
rupt himself. The idea here is to admit that self-corruption
will take place only in the presence of a kind of ignorance
(obscurity about one's condition), but that this self-obscurity is *willed*, and thus is within the range of the person's
responsibility. And so despair can exist as a self-corruption
(psychologically) for which a person is responsible (morally) only because the person "seeks by his own effort to
preserve an obscurity about his condition." Does this make
sense? If he seeks to remain obscure about himself, must he
not already know himself? Must he not know that he is trying not to know, and thus fail? These questions have been
dealt with by philosophers under the heading of self-deception (Kierkegaard uses the terms "double-mindedness,"
"cleverness," "self-deceit").[5]

   To think about self-deception is, at least at first, to confront an absurdity. It goes something like this. For me to deceive you, I intentionally do or say something in order to get
you to believe something that I do not believe. So if I
have successfully deceived you about a proposition "P," it
means (1) I believe "P" is true; (2) I do something that I
think will induce you to believe "P" is false; and (3) as a
result of what I did, you come to believe "P" is false. But if
I try to transfer this *inter*personal analysis of deception to an
*intra*personal case of *self*-deception, we seem to find problems. In the case of me and you the end result was that I believed "P" and you did not. In the intrapersonal case the end
result would be that I believed "P" and I did not. In the case
of me and you, I intended to get you to believe something I
knew was false. How could I intentionally try to get myself
to believe something which at the same time I knew to be
false? This has led some philosophers to conclude that self-deception is impossible. But any half-decent novelist or any
close observer of human life knows that self-deception not
only exists, but is pervasive. So the questions should not be
whether it exists, but how to account for it, and what false

presuppositions would lead someone to the claim that it does not exist. Let's see if we can make a start. Our account relies upon the following features of what we call *believing*: first, that believing is the making of a commitment; second, that there is a natural tendency not to believe ideas which cause us pain; third, that there is a natural tendency to believe ideas which are well supported by evidence; and finally, that anxiety results from going against any of these natural tendencies.

First, to believe an idea is different from merely entertaining that idea, rather like getting married is different from what is called "casual dating." When you get married you bring the other person into your life, as a part of your life. When you decide to believe an idea you have previously only entertained, you are saying that you are the kind of person who would espouse this idea. Therefore, depending upon the kind of belief involved, to decide to believe something is more or less to affirm who and what you are. Beliefs, then, are not intellectual entities which you *receive*, but decisions about yourself which you *make*.

Let's take the extreme case to make it clear. Think of a person who sees himself as a hard-nosed, practical, down-to-earth, profit-minded, successful businessman. What must take place before he would come to believe that the Marxist analysis of history and of contemporary affairs is true? Surely there must be the *cognitive* activity of coming to understand the Marxist analysis, its defenders and its critics. But this cognitive activity is never enough. Thousands just like him understand the same things and yet do not believe. More important, it cannot be enough because he cannot come to believe the Marxist analysis and remain the same person he is. For him to believe the Marxist analysis, he must also change his image of himself. There must then be a *volitional* activity of deciding to accept the Marxist analysis as part of his life and thus to *become* a different sort of person than he was. If he still reads *Forbes* magazine he experiences it differently. If he still goes to the country club he feels differently about it, etc. To believe is therefore to entertain, and then to commit. The committing is an *action* which the person *decides* to do. Like any other action we have a *great deal of control* over whether we take the step or not. We have a great deal of control over what we believe.

To this last point you may object. Suppose, you say, I adore my husband and before my eyes he is struck and killed by an automobile. I want to believe that he is still alive; it tortures me to believe that the body lying on the street is his, and is dead; and yet I have no control over what I believe. I cannot *decide* to believe that he is not dead. To this I would answer first that it was never claimed that a normal person can or should believe only what he *wants* to believe. This would be to ignore the cognitive half of what Kierkegaard refers to as the "dialectical interplay of knowledge and will." But secondly, even in the case you described you would try *for a time* to avoid the obvious belief, to withhold your commitment to the belief that your husband is dead. You must be dreaming. You pray, for the first time in years. You talk to your husband even though you "know" he is dead. You scream, "This can't be happening," etc. Maybe, just maybe, you will succeed *permanently* in not committing yourself to the dreadful belief, by simply refusing to do so. That *is* within your power, and the fact that you would then be labeled "insane" does little to clarify what it is you have done. We often say of such a person that they "cracked," that their mind somehow collapsed. But in fact what seems to have happened is more like the person who in the face of pressure simply folds his arms and announces that he will not budge an inch further. The problem is more one of too much control than one of loss of control.

This example illustrates also our second and third points about believing; namely that there is a natural tendency to commit oneself to ideas which are well supported, and another tendency to avoid ideas which are painful. The tendency to believe ideas which are well supported could easily be explained in an evolutionary fashion by focusing on the survival value of such a trait. It could be explained developmentally by the way we train children to accept beliefs supported in certain ways, and reject those supported in other ways. In any case the tendency is there, more or less like a habit, and whenever we try to go against it we will experience anxiety. And so as the normal person tries to deny the (obvious) death of a loved one by, for example, trying to believe that it is a dream, there is a "pull" back to reality. It is what Freud referred to as the "reality principle." How hard in general will a person resist that pull? It depends in part upon the painfulness of the belief he is trying to avoid, in part upon the amount of evidence the belief has, and ultimately upon the individual himself. The dialectic of cognition and will, involved in belief, is roughly something like this. If the belief is a pleasure to believe and well supported, there is no problem. If it is painful but with no support, there is no problem. If it is a pleasure but has little support, there is a problem. If it is painful but has adequate support, there is a problem, and so forth. If the belief makes little difference to me one way or the other, no problem arises.

Let's return then to the question of self-deception. Suppose I am a father who takes credit (and blame) for the actions and accomplishments of my children. I am proud when they are successful; guilty and ashamed when they fail. I begin to notice some items in my teenage daughter's room which I did not buy for her, and which she could not have purchased on her allowance. "My friend Helen lent them to me," she says, which seems odd to me. I notice more things, coats, jewelry, and I note that she spends a great deal of time at the shopping mall. She's looking for a job, I theorize. I know that one of her friends was recently convicted for shoplifting, but my daughter has always tried to help other kids in trouble. I bring to mind that time when she was ten, how she befriended the girl in her class that no one liked. I shouldn't be going into her room at home anyway; she deserves privacy at her age. Perhaps that summer tennis camp we talked about a few years ago would be good for her. Everyone should have at least one "lifetime sport."

When they call to say that they are holding her at the department store, I know right away what has happened. I always told her that her weakness for the underdog, for the child in trouble, would someday come to haunt her. Now she's been dragged into a mess because she was with the girl when she was shoplifting again. That settles it for the tennis camp, no matter what it costs. I always told her she was too passive in the face of strong personalities. The fact that she was in possession of stolen goods outside the store means nothing. As I said, she's always been very gullible. She was obviously just holding them for that little thief she's been with lately. The photographic record of her leaving the store with stolen clothing doesn't mean she's really a thief. It was probably a dare, a child's prank. And so it goes. . . .

But finally the "break" comes (probably). "My child is a thief," I say, and it hurts. I have maneuvered to avoid that hurt for months. As the evidence piles up, the pressure on

me to increase the sophistication of my maneuvers becomes
too great. Finally I have run out of tricks. I have to either
give up and accept the hurt, or cross the boundary—that is,
fold my arms and deny the cognitive demands of the dialectic. Was I deceiving myself all these months? Most assuredly
I was, and I can tell by just asking myself how I would have
believed if the potential of the hurt had not been there, if it
had been someone else's child. Self-deception is the refusal to
commit myself to a belief because of the pain of that commitment, where had that pain not been present the commitment would have been made as a natural expression of the
tendency to believe well-supported ideas.

But there is still a problem here. To say I was deceiving
myself all those months is to say that I was in possession of
the "theory" that my daughter was a thief, and that I was
maneuvering to avoid committing myself to that theory. But
if I was maneuvering in this way I must have known that I
was doing it, and thus I must have "known" that the
"shoplifting theory" was the best-supported theory, otherwise I would not have maneuvered to avoid it. Thus the
very fact that I was maneuvering seems to indicate that the
maneuver, to avoid the idea of my daughter as a thief,
would fail. Yet for all those months it didn't fail. How is
that so?

It is to answer this question that Freud introduced the
"topographic" division of the personality into the "regions"
of conscious, preconscious, and unconscious. He could thus
say that the maneuvers (e.g., defense mechanisms) were
done intentionally but unconsciously. This turned out to be
a fruitful idea, but not, I think, necessary. The perplexity
rests upon the assumption that every time I am maneuvering to avoid something I must be *at that time* thinking about
what it is I am trying to avoid. But this is surely not true. I
drive a car in such a way as to avoid an accident, but this
does not mean that I am at all times thinking about myself
in an auto accident as I drive. I develop habits to avoid having my city apartment burgled, but I do not have "before
my mind" the possible burglary every time I lock the door.
Finally, I have had an argument with a lover and am now
"trying to avoid her." I prearrange my schedule to avoid
seeing her, as well as to avoid ideas and memories of her. I
keep busy, go skiing, make sure I have plenty of friends
around, drink more than usual, take on extra projects at

work, go to the movies, etc. This entire change in my established pattern could be truly characterized as "maneuvering to avoid thinking about my former lover." It may very well be successful, which would mean that because of my maneuvers I did not think about her very much. Thus, the fact that I maneuver to avoid something clearly does not imply that I am at that time thinking about it.

So all those times that I did not go into my daughter's room as I normally would have, I was maneuvering to avoid the belief that she was a shoplifter. But that does not imply that I was thinking at those times about the fact that she was a shoplifter. I was thinking about whatever it was I was doing in lieu of being in her room, grouting the tiles in the bathroom which I had been putting off for two years.

To summarize, when I deceive myself I maneuver to avoid (1) the pain of accepting a particular new belief as *my belief*, (2) the pain of resisting a well-established belief, by concocting an alternative hypothesis, or rationalization, and trying to support that as successfully as the painful belief, and (3) the pain involved in the belief that I am maneuvering and thus being a dishonest person. The fact that I am maneuvering indicates that the painful idea has been seriously entertained, and in that sense it is true to say of the self-deceiver that he knows "deep down" what he is doing.[6] But the fact that I am maneuvering does not mean that I am thinking about what I am avoiding as I am avoiding it. And thus the maneuver *can succeed*, since the pain is present only when I am thinking about it. In self-deception I am maneuvering to escape a truth about myself. I am a self divided against itself. This is the meaning of Kierkegaard's term "double-mindedness." The opposite of self-deception, of willing obscurity about oneself, is to be transparent to oneself. It is to will one thing. To be transparent to oneself requires insight and courage. Not to will transparency is to be a fool and a coward.

Let us return now to the question about despair. Despair is both a corruption of the self, and something for which we are (willfully) responsible. Socrates was right that only in ignorance could someone harm himself. But self-deception is a case of willed ignorance. Despair is possible only when a person is ignorant (obscure) about himself in a way which he himself arranges. And so as Kierkegaard says, the very nature of what despair is implies that the person is aware of his despair "but from this it does not follow that he . . . is himself conscious of it" [SUD, p. 163].

With this in mind we can now very briefly chart out Kierkegaard's description of the relationships between consciousness and despair. To begin, no normal person is completely unaware of his own despair, or what is the same, of the fact that he has (potentially) a self. Kierkegaard discussed "despair which is unconscious of being despair," but only in a relative sense. The major point is that the degree to which a person is unaware of his despair is the degree to which he is spiritless, and it is the degree to which he is furthest from possible help. A person who approximates this form of despair has no regard for insight or for truth. On the other hand, the degree to which a person is unaware of his own despair is the degree to which he is shielded from the tensions of genuine human life. Such a person is a pure ideal type. A person completely unconscious of despair would not be a person.

Once despair which is conscious (to some extent) is considered, Kierkegaard distinguishes between the despair of weakness and the despair of defiance. In the despair of weakness a person recognizes that he potentially has a self and yet does not dare to try to bring that self about. He gives up. In less reflective stages, stages in which the consciousness of despair is most successfully avoided, the person will transfer his disappointment about himself onto a disappointment over *things*. This Kierkegaard calls the despair over the earthly, and is the most common form of despair.

> Thus the self coheres with "the other," wishing, desiring, enjoying, etc., but passively. . . . Its dialectic is the agreeable and disagreeable; its concepts are good fortune, misfortune, fate. [SUD, p. 184]

When misfortune occurs, it is this over which he despairs, or so he thinks. He knows he has a self, that he has betrayed that self, but this knowledge is shunted aside by the "everyday."

> Despair over the earthly or over something earthly is the commonest sort of despair. . . . The more thoroughly reflected the despair is, the more rarely it occurs in the world. . . . There are very few men who live even only passably in the category of spirit. . . .

> . . . the majority of men do never really manage
> in their whole life to be more than they were in
> childhood and youth, namely, immediacy with the
> addition of a little dose of self-reflection. [SUD, p.
> 190]

To live in the everyday, ground smooth as a pebble, dili-
gently worrying over the particulars of one's life, is the most
common tactic to avoid oneself. There are those, however,
who acquire a more acute awareness of the nature of
despair, of the self, of the fact that the self is being wasted
and abused. Rather than take action, though, they give up
hope that they can ever become a self. The despair *of*
weakness takes the form of the despair *over* weakness. They
try but they can't get away from themselves, that is, from
the consciousness of having failed themselves.

> As it often was the case with the father who disin-
> herited his son that the outward fact was of little
> avail to him, he did not by this get free of his son
> . . . so it is in the case of the despairing self with
> relation to itself. [SUD, p. 196]

For this person the normal tricks of diversion simply do not
work. The most he can do is retreat further and further into
himself. Translators of Kierkegaard have used the English
terms "introversion," "close reserve," and "shut-up-ness" to
describe this phenomenon. But while the person retreats into
himself, so also he fears and avoids solitude, or any other situation which would lead to self-reflection.

> If on the other hand he talks to someone, if to one
> single man he opens his heart, he is in all probabil-
> ity strained to so high a tension, or so much let
> down, that suicide does not result from introversion.
> [SUD, p. 200]

And yet "talking it out" is not without its dangers, as would
be obvious from the fact that the defenses *were* put there to
begin with for a reason. "There are examples of introverts
who are brought to despair precisely because they have acquired a confidant" [SUD, p. 200]. And of course there is
the possibility that the person will attempt to avoid this
despair by regression.

> . . . he will seek forgetfulness in sensuality, perhaps
> in debauchery, in desperation he wants to return to

immediacy, but constantly with consciousness of the self, which he does not want to have. [SUD, p. 199]

These are all forms of the despair of weakness, because the person is attempting to escape from the fact that he has an eternal self, a fact of which he is more or less conscious. The most intense and highly developed form of despair is the despair of defiance, "the despair of willing despairingly to be oneself." In this case a person attempts on his own to *create* a self. Far from attempting to avoid being a self, he sees it as his right, ability, and obligation to construct a self, *ex nihilo*. His demand is always that he be allowed to do it on his own. "That is to say he is not willing to begin with the beginning, but 'in the beginning.'" But this, Kierkegaard says, is not possible. Without a conception of the necessary in me, of who I am already, no genuine self can emerge. Any *pose* which I adopt would have equal claim to be me as any other pose. Thus the defiant one becomes master of himself, but

> . . . this ruler is a king without a country, he rules really over nothing; his condition, his dominion, is subjected to the dialectic that every instant revolution is legitimate. For in the last resort this depends arbitrarily upon the self. . . . So the despairing self is constantly building castles in the air. [SUD, p. 203][8]

In his book *The Concept of Dread*, Kierkegaard refers to the despair of defiance as the demoniacal, defining the demonic as fear of the good. Where what the despair of weakness most detested and feared was its own evil, the demonic fears most what is ultimately the source of his salvation as a person. The phenomenon in psychiatric circles is known as resistance. Kierkegaard's theory is that in fearing to be "touched" by a helper, by goodness of any kind, he attempts to pollute everything he touches to prove that existence is without goodness. He can even use himself as an attempt to proves that evil pervades reality. He becomes evil, the sadist, the demonic. "The demonic despair is the most potentiated form of the despair which despairingly wills to be itself" [SUD, p. 207].

This overview of despair, its forms, its motives, its technique, has been necessarily brief. Meat will be placed on the bones of the theory in Part II of this book. Let's consider in summary form the points of the last two chapters.

1. The person is, from an ethically relevant perspective, a synthesis of opposing elements. This synthesis is not achieved naturally but is willed by the person. Because it is a synthesis there is a natural tendency for the human self to break apart, a tendency which is resisted only by the constant effort of the human will.

2. The tendency of the self to break apart is motivated by dread (anxiety), which is the natural reaction of the person to the fact that the future is to some extent under his control (and to some extent not). As a response to the possibility of freedom, dread is a completely ambivalent reaction, a reaction at once of attraction and repulsion.

3. To be a self is to be free, which is to hold together and dialectically opposing elements of the self in the face of the dread (anxiety) which this entails. Because life changes, situations change, and the self must change, there can be no rules, no paths to follow concerning whether or not the elements of the self are in proper relationship. Were there such rules life would be a rational, mechanical process and dread would be nonexistent.

4. To escape anxiety is therefore to escape from being a self. It is to be in despair. No mode of life, system of belief, program of personal growth, or form of therapy which promises to extinguish anxiety can be successful if the point is also to be a self. To be human is to be anxious, to live in uncertainty, to risk failure, to exercise will.

5. Despair is, therefore, the condition of the human self when its elements are not properly related. In its most general scheme it is either to live in infinitude and deny finitude or the reverse. Despair is a condition of the entire human self, psychological as well as moral. It is psychological in that it is, for example, a state of hypersensitivity, or loss of contact with reality, or total immersion in the minute details of the everyday, etc. It is moral in that it is the choice not to be what one

should be. From the moral perspective despair is sin.

6. To say that despair is sin is to imply that it is the person's responsibility. Psychologically it is sickness. Morally it is sin. This implies that it is a *chosen* sickness. How could a person choose to be sick? The answer is through the strategies of self-deception, where self-deception is the willful avoidance of a painful belief. It is in the last analysis a willful attempt to remain obscure about oneself.

7. To be transparent to oneself, to eschew self-deception even in the face of dread, requires courage. To despair is to be a coward. The concepts of courage and cowardice, which have no place in a deterministic account of human life, are essential to any account which recognizes human freedom. To describe the strategies of defense through self-deception is to describe the modes of applied cowardice.

There is one implication of our discussion of self-deception which can be noted here before we close Part I of the book. We began the discussion of self-deception by noting that you believe what you believe not because it has been forced upon you, but rather because you have chosen. To believe, we said, is rather like getting married. It is a commitment which says something about who you are. How much it says about this is a guide to how important the belief is. It is within your power to *not* believe most of what you do believe, though it may not be in your power to do it rationally. It still remains as Kierkegaard says, that in all belief there is a dialectic of knowing and willing. This means that there is a personal, subjective element in all belief, and especially in those "belief systems" or "value systems" which we cherish so dearly. No important or interesting theory can ever be "proven" beyond the powers of an individual to doubt, and most cannot be proven beyond a *reasonable* doubt. This does not imply that you can believe what you want. But it does imply that what you believe (Catholic, Communist, Moslem, Republican, atheist, patriot, traitor, etc.) is your responsibility. It is within your power, as a free agent, to change these fundamental beliefs and so change yourself. If this were not true, the idea of despair would be senseless, as would the idea of self-deception. Also senseless would be the project which Kierkegaard set for his life.[9]

We are now in a position to apply these thoughts to specific cases, styles of living, to see whether they will yield fruit. This is the task of the next part of the book.

II.

APPLICATION

SIX

THE INDIVIDUAL—
IN ONE DIMENSION

The first five chapters have prepared the historical and theoretical background for what is to follow. These chapters have described two competing intellectual traditions, the most basic two traditions of Kierkegaard's time. But Kierkegaard was too serious a person to be interested in intellectual traditions as ideas. He was interested in them as *ways to live.* One way to live is to stress your own satisfaction or fulfillment *as an individual* whose entire existence is confined to the *everyday world,* that is, in one dimension. It is the life lived according to individualist humanist principles. Kierkegaard referred to it as the aesthetic life, but the word "aesthete" was normally associated with its most sophisticated practitioner, the romantic, or the ironist. As a life view, though, it encompasses many different levels of sophistication. Some of these will be discussed in this chapter.

Another way to live is to stress your position in relation to other people. It is to seek satisfaction or fulfillment *through the group* whose entire existence is confined to the everyday, that is, in one dimension. The group referred to is any form of human relatedness, for example, family, friendships, professions, political associations, fraternal organizations, and so forth. Kierkegaard called this the ethical life and associated it with a bourgeois ideology, the most sophisticated justification for which he found in Hegelianism. Kierkegaard's evaluation and critique of this as a way of life is found in Chapter Seven, titled "The Group—in One Dimension."

It would not be possible for Kierkegaard to evaluate these ways of living if he did not have himself some theory of what a human being is, of what life holds for a person in the optimum, of what it means for a person to be corrupted *as a person*. Chapters Four and Five presented Kierkegaard's views on these questions in a preliminary fashion, enough at least to allow for an evaluation of the views mentioned. Both views, he will argue, if carried through even in the ideal, represent despair, a structural disrelationship within the self. Neither life is worthy of a commitment by a human being. Only a two-dimensional life can do justice to the dignity which is human life. What this means must wait until Chapter Eight.

We begin with a discussion of the idea of a one-dimensional life of individual self-realization. But we don't go directly to romanticism, because that is only its most clever variation. We will begin rather at its simplest and least sophisticated version and work our way up.

a. The Beautiful People

> In his younger days the Count had had a diplomatic post, he was now elderly. . . . The Countess had been extraordinarily beautiful as a young girl, as an elderly person she was still the most beautiful woman I have ever seen. The Count in his youth had great success with the fair sex because of his manly beauty. . . . Old age had not broken him, and a noble, genuinely superior dignity made him still more goodlooking. . . . Both the Count and the Countess were highly cultivated, and yet the life view of the Countess was concentrated in the thought that they were the handsomest couple in the whole land. [E/O, II, p. 185–6]

This is the bourgeois Hegelian Judge William speaking, describing a certain type of focus which one may adopt for one's life. Here one centers a life upon the physical characteristics of health and beauty.

> Here we have a view of life which teaches that health is the most precious good, that on which everything hinges. The same view acquires a more poetic expression when it is said that beauty is the

highest. Now beauty is a very fragile good, and
therefore one seldom sees this view carried through.
One encounters often enough a young girl (or
maybe a young man) who for a brief time prides
herself upon her beauty, but soon it deceives her.
[E/O, II, p. 187]

Physical health and beauty are factors over which the individual has very little control in the short run, and none in
the long run. To use Kierkegaard's language, they lie outside
of the realm of freedom. A life organized around these principles is an *immediate* (spiritless) life, different from the life
of the animal only in the insignificant sense that it is *in a way*
an attempt to improve upon nature. But sickness and the decay of physical beauty are inexorable, and so in the long run
this life resembles the child's sandcastles built to hold back
the incoming tide. Because this life is organized around a
center which is not within the realm of freedom, great emphasis is placed upon fate and its two sides, fortune and misfortune. This means that when you find yourself or your
life "out of control" all you can do is wait. You must let
"fate" take its course. Perhaps things will turn out well (fortune) or perhaps badly (misfortune).

Your life is in these circumstances one of waiting and
watching, as when the brakes of your car fail and you are
out of control. If your entire life is organized around a principle which is not in your control, then your life is one of
waiting and watching. You hope for fortune, you fear the
prospect of misfortune. Even though one's life may be "active" in the area of health spas, dieting, organic foods, running, leg lifts, face lifts, fashion design, situps, pushups, tennis,
etc., essentially it is the life of *waiting*, waiting for the inexorable (necessity) and for the sudden (chance), "for fate is precisely the unity of necessity and chance" [CD, p. 87]. When
either "befalls" him, his response is to wish to be someone
else.

To think of this awhile is to realize its absuridty and its
sadness. I wish that I had lived in the time of Socrates. Is
that even conceivable? Think of someone of whom you
might say, "That is me, living then." What does that person
have in common with you? He surely can't think like you
(he's never even read Kierkegaard—nor Plato for that matter), nor remember, feel, react, behave, or anything else like
you, and so on. But the "immediate" person identifies self

with factors so inessential to his spirit (health, beauty) that
to wish to be another self resembles wishing to have another's clothes, or face, or build, or health. "For the immediate man does not recognize his self, he recognizes himself
only by his dress. . . . There is no more ludicrous confusion" [SUD, p. 187]. It is also sad and comic, as when the
middle-aged strain to appear young, the fat strain to appear
thin, the ugly glamorous. No one is degraded more than he
who provokes that curious mixture of laughter and pity
which accompanies such attempts. To attempt to live out
this life of health and beauty is to inevitably become
obsessed with its enemies—physical decay, disease, and death.

A culture containing this life-style in significant num-
bers can expect its institutions to reflect this fact. Hypochondria will be the prevailing neurosis. Literature on
health, disease, death, dying, cure, and miracles will be devoured. The warriors against death (the doctors), the makers
of miracles, will take on the character of priests, the forces
of good in battle against evil (disease, death). And one's
body, that is one's self, will be handed over to these priests
to work their ministrations.[1] One could expect also "saviors"
who would preach that the inexorable can be avoided, as
when one hopes for the medical elimination of death, or
faith cures. In more symbolic forms, the jogging, running,
marathoning craze points in this direction. Exorbitant claims
of "permanent protection against heart attack" (male death)
or reversal of the aging process have reached ludicrous
proportions even within the "medical community." One
would expect guilt in this realm to center around bodily
abuse (so-called "junk" food, fat, sickness) and the rites of
purification and punishment to involve one's body (fasting,
"natural" foods, and most extreme, in running, "pushing
through the pain barrier"). The analogies with orthodox religion are endless.

The Countess, of Judge William's acquaintance, has so
organized her life. And on its own terms she has been emi-
nently successful. She is able to say in her old age,

> Little William, my Deltev, is surely the handsomest
> man in the whole kingdom, is he not? Yes I can see
> well enough that he has sunk together a little bit on
> one side, but no one can see that when I am walking
> with him, and when we walk together we are surely
> the handsomest couple in the whole land. [E/O, II,
> p. 186]

Do you detect in the Countess a certain simplemindedness born perhaps of self-deception? This possibility has not escaped the observant Kierkegaard.

> The fact that the external is not always the internal is not only true with respect to the ironists, who consciously deceive others with a false exterior, but it is also true quite often with respect to immediate natures, who unconsciously deceive themselves, yes sometimes have almost a need for self-deception.[2]

What must the Countess think on those long nights with the Count beside her, content in his dreams? Can her thoughts only touch upon the next day's promenade? Or on days of past beauty? What must she think when presented with life's cruelties, the suffering of others, or her own impending decay? How can she sustain her optimism? The answer: only by slipping further and further into reverie, into despair. Having chosen to base a life on a characteristic over which she has no final *concrete* control, she can succeed only in her dreams. The Countess has no concrete freedom within the life she has chosen. She must succumb to the despair of necessity in which she says, "I am what I am; whatever will come, will come." Having resigned her concrete life to fate, she retreats into the infinitude of her dreams in which "whatever I wish to come, will come." Does the Countess have no real choices? Not within the life she has chosen; a life which rests upon self-deception, a life which is despair. Is her despair conscious? Only in that instant when the thought steals its way through a crack and into her mind. "Your life is nothing," it says and is quickly smothered. What reaction time she has! It is only this which sustains her.

b. Wealth and Standing

> His motto is: Every man's a thief in his business. "It is impossible," says he, "to be able to get through this world if one is not just like the other. . . ." As for religion—well, really his religion is this: Every man's a thief in his business. He also has a religion in addition to this, and his opinion is that every tradesman ought to have one. . . . he explains that

the Jews always have the reputation of cheating
more than the Christians which, as he maintains, is
by no means the case; he maintains that the Christians cheat just as well as the Jews, but what injures
the Jews is the fact that they do not have the religion which prevails in the land. [AC, p. 206]

[Similarly] He has now, as they say in romances,
been happily married for a number of years, is an
active and enterprising man, a father and a citizen,
perhaps even a great man; at home in his own house
the servants speak of him as "himself," in the city he
is among the honoraries; his bearing suggests "respect of persons." . . . In Christendom he is a Christian (quite in the same sense in which in paganism
he would have been a pagan, and in England an En-
glishman), one of the cultured Christians. . . .
more than once he has asked the parson whether
there really was such an immortality, whether one
would really recognize oneself again—which indeed
must have for him a very singular interest, since he
has no self. [SUD, p. 189–90]

From the point of view of whether or not one is a self,
and the kind and degree of one's despair, these two life plans
are identical. Of course the tradesman thinks the Countess is
lazy and self-indulgent and the latter thinks the tradesman a
bit vulgar, but both are essentially the same. They center
their lives upon something external to the self and something
by and large outside of the realm of freedom. If one gives
herself to the physical (health, beauty), the other gives himself to the material (wealth, fame). To own the world is to
be owned by the world. Both are spiritless, and strive to remain so.

> . . . he treats with great precaution the bit of self-
> reflection which he has in himself, he is afraid this
> thing in the background might emerge. [SUD, p.
> 189]

Externally, *at least,* he is you or I.

> . . . in representing spiritlessness one commonly
> puts into the mouth of the character sheer
> twaddle. . . . In fact, spirit-lessness can utter the
> same words the richest spirit has uttered, only it does
> not utter them by virtue of spirit. Man when he is
> characterized as spiritless has become a talking
> machine, and there is nothing to prevent him from

learning a philosophical rigmarole just as easily as a confession of faith and a political recitative. . . . [CD, p. 85]

Spiritless man is a chatterer, solitude presents him with a threat. Spiritual man can endure isolation, "whereas we men are constantly in need of 'the other,' the herd; we die, or despair, if we are not reassured by being in the herd, of the same opinion as the herd, etc." [AC, p. 163].

In the above two classes falls the "everyman" of contemporary life. About this person you would say there is nothing extraordinary. This person is the Philistine. Kierkegaard's views of the "everyman" and of his life were most clearly stated in a short work with a long title, *Two Ages: The Age of Revolution and the Present Age, A Literary Review*. It is on the surface a review of a novel by Christine Cryllenbourg-Ehrensuard. The novel describes two love affairs separated by a generation. The first took place against the backdrop of the romantic revolutionary era of the late eighteenth century; the French Revolution was still fresh. Claudine conceives her lover Lusard's child out of wedlock; is unavoidably separated from him for nine passionately faithful years; and is finally reunited in a true "repetition." The second affair took place during "the present age" of the mid-nineteenth century. Marione and Ferdinand are young and in love; the match is opposed by her father; after interminable discussion the couple sensibly decides that financial difficulties preclude their union; the day is suddenly saved by the younger Lusard's offer of money, achieving a repetition (of sorts). This story is retold in Part I of the review. Part II offers an aesthetic appreciation of what and how the author has accomplished an artistic description of the two ages through the example of domestic life. In Part III Kierkegaard extends the analysis of the work under review in a brilliant description of "the present age."

> The present age is essentially a sensible, reflecting age, devoid of passion, flaring up in superficial, short-lived enthusiasm and prudentially relaxing in indolence. [TA, p. 68]

This sets the cornerstone of the analysis. There are some superficial quips about young people expiring before the deliberation concerning suicide was completed (in contrast presumably to all those melancholic young people who ended it all clutching copies of *Werther*); of a generation in which it is obligatory to be a legal expert; of a politician who called a meeting to vote upon whether to have a revolution; of theological students who would find self-denial inconceivable but who would easily "found a social institution with no less a goal than to save all who are lost" [JA, p. 71]. In a passionate age if a treasure were discovered far out on thin ice, the crowd would remain in safe territory cheering

> . . . the brave person who skates out on the thin ice. They would shudder for him and with him in his perilous decision, would grieve for him if he meets his death, and would idealize him if he gets the treasure. [TA, p. 72]

Not so in "the present age." The venture would be declared imprudent. But for the amusement of all and with their knowledge, a forgery would be staged, "an *inspired venture* would be transformed into an *acrobatic* stunt" [TA, p. 72]. The most accomplished skater would pretend to skate near the edge, remaining always out of danger, turning "actuality into a theater." But far from edifying the participants—as in the case of true heroism—it would have the opposite effect.

> . . . the celebrators would go home more disposed than ever to the most dangerous but also the most aristocratic of all diseases, to admire socially what one personally regards as trivial, because the whole thing had become a theatrical joke. . . . [TA, p. 73]

The point is that once concrete, passionate, and meaningful actions have been transformed, emptied of meaning, and remain only as caricatures of themselves. When this happens, life becomes theater. What better way to describe the tendency in the present age toward "media events," "Super Sundays," the political life of "unannounced candidates," "trial balloons," "state of the world messages," the social science of "role models," "dramaturgical selves," "games," "social roles"—the list is endless. What these have in common is the expression of behavior which lacks the meaning of inwardness, form without content, or more specifically the equation of content and form. The effect can only be as Kierkegaard says, a dispirited cynicism and a vague longing for something genuine.

This is not to deny that "the present age" is revolutionary. It is an age in which fundamental shifts in human life are taking place. But these shifts occur while allowing everything to *seem* to remain as is. "The present age"

> . . . lets everything remain but subtly drains the meaning out of it; rather than culminating in an uprising, it exhausts the inner actuality of relations in a tension of reflection that lets everything remain and yet has transformed the whole of existence into an equivocation. . . . [TA, p. 77]

Genuine human relationships necessarily involve a tension (*pace* Hegel); they are "coiled springs" binding qualitatively different and unequal persons. Not so in "the present age." Whereas previously a citizen acknowledged and paid homage to his leader, now

> . . . the citizen does not relate himself in the relation but is a spectator computing the problem: the relation of a subject to his king. [TA, p. 79]

The father does not impart his authority upon the respectful child. Rather "the relation itself becomes a problem in which the parties like rivals in a game watch each other." The relationship of teacher and student becomes "a certain uniformity in mutual exchange between teacher and pupil on how a good school should be run" [TA, p. 79].

There is described here a vast emptying out of the "coiled springs" of once passionate relationships and with it of tension, fervor, and enthusiasm, replaced by chatter about "social roles," "open marriage," "marriage encounters," "open-ended commitments," talking therapies, and pop-psych manuals. "In Germany there are even handbooks for lovers . . . there are handbooks for everything" [TA, p. 104].

The consequence of this draining process which changes everything while allowing it to seem to remain the same is a vast social universe of equivocation. Once polar opposites, absolute "either/ors," are now collapsed into meaningless and degrading "mediations."

> What is it *to chatter?* It is the annulment of the passionate disjunction between being silent and speaking. Only the person who can remain essentially silent can speak essentially, can act essentially. [TA, p. 97]

To have made the distinction between appropriate silence
and appropriate speech is to distinguish in oneself the private
(me) from the public (we). The chatterer blurts out everything with his "trivial rattling" and "garrulous confiding."
Chattering is the "caricaturing externalization of inwardness."

> What is formlessness? It is the annulled passionate
> distinction between form and content. . . . [TA, p.
> 100]

Instead of life expressing in action a deeply held orientation,
it becomes an aimless sampling, a "philandering among great
diversities." It is a life in which as the commercial says, "You
only go around once, so you have to grab all the gusto you
can."

> What is superficiality and its characteristic propen-
> sity: "the exhibitionist tendency?" Superficiality is
> the annulled passionate distinction between hid-
> denness and revelation. It is the revelation of
> emptiness. . . . [TA, p. 102]

In the present age we refer to this person as "open," "honest," and anyone else as "repressed," "uptight." Sit next to
him on a train and you will quickly learn how he feels about
you, his mother, his "relationships": and how he feels about
the fact that he feels this way about you, his mother, and his
"relationships."

> What is philandering? It is the annulled passionate
> distinction between loving and being essentially de-
> bauched. [TA, p. 102]

In the present age the essential human commitment of marriage is being whittled from both ends. Nonmarital relationships imitate marriage, while marital relationships—under the
ruse of "open marriage," "nonpossessivist commitments,"
etc.—imitate nonmarriage. Lacking the will to either dispense
with or enter into actual marriage. modern man reflects,
dodges, and chatters about such "mediations" as "nonbinding
commitments." It was the mind-set of one who could use the
latter expression with a straight face that Kierkegaard at-
tacked when he complained of the annulment of the principle of contradiction. On this point Christopher Lasch has
recently said:

The humanist psychologies of Rogers, May, and Maslow, widely diffused by such best sellers as the O'Neills' *Open Marriage* and the Francoeurs' *Hot and Cool Sex*, converges with pop sociology in a defense of monogamy that ingeniously incorporates a bitter attack upon the family.[3]

Lasch is here making Kierkegaard's point. The attack upon marriage contained in such approaches is not direct; it does not reject the language of "marriage," "husband," "commitment," etc., but it does alter drastically the meanings of these terms. As a result a commitment can now be "nonbinding," whereas previously that would have been akin to characterizing a square as circular. With this view of marriage gaining credence, it does not seem so ludicrous to hear from Lewis Yablonsky that most philandering husbands claimed to have "good-excellent" home lives and that their extramarital sex in fact improved their marriages. This would be ludicrous only if marriage were understood as a moral institution resting upon love, mutual trust, and binding promises. Were the latter to be the case, a marriage in which one partner systematically violated the trust would be a cruel joke. This is true irrespective of whether the other partner is aware.[4]

It should not be surprising then that the divorce rate is approaching 40 percent. It is increasingly common today that the desertion of spouse and children is adequately justified by an appeal solely to one's own individual "happiness," "growth," or "career." Having freely and consciously entered into promises and commitments which drastically affect the lives of spouse and children, people increasingly walk away from these promises with the justification "I wasn't growing as a person." Any feelings of remorse associated with this are considered "guilts" to be dealt with in "therapy." Whereas for Kierkegaard marriage presented an either/or (either you make and keep the promises that define marriage, or you do not get married), the present age clamors for a both/and.

It is still possible to be parent or child, leader or follower, married or single, religious or secular, student or teacher, etc., but only in a way which represents a pale copy of the "coiled springs" of past relationships. There has been a vast "leveling" of distinctions, a democratizing and thus destruction of every significant social relationship, every

position of authority, every natural elite. The attitudes
which are essential to the genuineness of the relationships are
missing. With the bond of inwardness missing, commercial
considerations become predominant. As Marx pointed out at
about the same time in *The German Ideology,* bourgeois
relations resolve finally into matters of economic utility.
Why else does the present age not blink an ethical eye as
students sue teachers, lovers sue their former mates, husbands and wives sue each other, patients sue doctors, clients
sue their lawyers? And recently "the present age" was
blessed with the first malpractice suit by a child against his
parents. To justify this "leveling" of the inequalities which
are natural to most human relationships,

> ... a phantom must first be raised, the spirit of lev-
> eling, a monstrous abstraction, an all-encompassing
> something that is nothing, a mirage—and this phan-
> tom is *the public.* [TA, p. 90]

Along with the public is created *the press* as its spokesman
and teacher. Having destroyed the fundamental interhuman
distinctions and devoured the intrahuman distinction between privacy and revelation, the present age considers everything in the open, as fit topic for chatter and gossip.

> ... the present age is an age of publicity, the age
> of miscellaneous announcements: nothing happens
> but still there is instant publicity. [TA, p. 70]

The "gallery public" devours the gossip and begins to believe that "everything anyone does is done so that it (the
public) may have something to gossip about" [TA, p. 94], as
if, for example, citizens began to believe that whatever a politician did or said was geared toward how it would appear
to the "gallery-public."

In this age of publicity the most intimate secrets, secrets
no one would care to disclose in private, are eagerly "put in
writing for the public, and to be known by the public as
public" [TA, p. 100]. In the present age public figures write
books about their sex lives, politicians' wives about their
face lifts, children about the cruelty of their now dead
parents, lovers about their affairs with now dead presidents,
paraplegics about the fight to control their bowels—all justified, of course, on the principle of the "public's right to
know."

"The age of revolution is essentially passionate and therefore also has a concept of propriety" [TA, p. 64]. "The present age" is vulgar precisely because it is without passion. The polar opposite of the vulgar is the sacred, but without inwardness and passion, nothing is sacred. The double meaning of "profane" as on the one hand obscene and on the other hand secular is no accident, and ours is a most profane age.

The above cannot be dismissed with the magical incantations of "reactionary" or "antidemocratic." Kierkegaard was interested in only one matter, the spiritual condition of the individual. He saw in "the present age" a vast convergence of forces which threatened that spirit. Romanticism, Hegelianism, bourgeois Protestantism, the rise of mass (liberal) politics, social democratization, the rise of the press, urbanization, were some of these forces. He firmly believed that there were past eras more suitable for the development and exercise of the individual human spirit. In this sense he was a reactionary, but someone who is a reactionary *in no sense* would be guilty of a most foolish temporal chauvinism. It would be to believe that every area of human life is better today than it was yesterday.

The rise of liberal politics in the late eighteenth century threatened the individual primarily by engendering a view that human salvation was a *political problem*. This could escape the ludicrous only if salvation were defined in group/secular terms rather than individual/spiritual terms. This was the legacy of the enlightenment. Kierkegaard believed "the more insignificant a matter is, the more suitable it is to make a decision by voting" when the individual human spirit is the measure of significance. Kierkegaard's "politics" was not so much antidemocratic as antipolitical. It was an argument against the idea of politics as savior.

> The present age . . . is the opposite of the Reformation, which appeared to be a religious movement and proved to be political; now everything appears to be politics but will turn out to be a religious movement. [J&P, VI, p. 6256]

Kierkegaard sees then the life of the everyman in our "modern" age as one of cowardly self-indulgence. The attempt is always to take the easy course, and to concoct later the rationalizations to justify such cowardice.

> ... whereas a passionate age accelerates, raises up
> and overthrows, elevates and debases, a reflective
> apathetic age does the opposite, it stifles and
> impedes, it levels. [TA, p. 84]

Picture, then, a society in which its members are obsessed with physical well-being, attractiveness, and social place; with the position of the other relative to each; with the opinions of the other; the approval of the other, and with shaping one's own self to conform to the other. In this situation the other is not a person, or a hero (role model, in contemporary jargon), but rather an abstraction—"society," "the public." The public would speak through "the press" and be spoken to by the press. The ideas of the public would be canonized and polished by the press. This would be a society without privacy. The most intimate secrets of public figures would be relayed instantly to the public, as gossip and chatter. Indeed these figures would eagerly volunteer these secrets (for a price) to the public, which will just as eagerly pay. It would be a time of instant communication so that there is no gap between what the other is doing and the exercise of "the public's right to know." Politicians would play to the public as if on a stage; flatter, cajole, lie to the public, and steal from the public in full view *and knowledge* of the public, which will judge harshly only a failure to act out the role. Politicians will have no interest in governing; the point will be to become a governor. "Statesmanship in modern states is not: how one *manages to be* a cabinet minister, but: how one *manages to become* a cabinet minister" [J&P, IV, p. 4215]. And the art of becoming a governor in such a society will be radically different from the art of *being* a governor. But in a sense this incompetence, as well as the lack of talent and of character, in the politicians is irrelevant. It is a characteristic of this age that the evils of society focus upon the government. Journalists write and talk endlessly about the politicians, about "foreign affairs," and "domestic affairs," pretending to themselves and to the public that these "affairs," affect the individual and are important. The public watches as one would a soap opera, and joins the game. But the time of reform of government is passed; not because government is perfect but rather because there is a more urgent business.

Most people believe that taking a stand against the crowd is utter nonsense, for the crowd, the majority,

> the public are, after all, the saving powers, those
> freedom loving societies from which salvation shall
> issue—against kings and popes and public officials
> who want to tyrannize over us. . . . They do not
> dream that historical categories change and that now
> the crowd is and will be the only tyrant and the root
> corruption. . . . [J&P, IV, p. 4118]

It follows that reform of the crowd takes precedence over
reform of government. And of course this is not to be done
through government, or through law. It is a characteristic of
this age that all problems are handled through government,
all disputes are settled through law. Government cannot reform the crowd, for the problems of the crowd—the problems of cowardice, self-deception, willful ignorance, envy,
fear, and emptiness—are not amenable to legislative solution.

Does this imply that nothing should be done about the
"great problems of our day," war, injustice, inflation, racism,
inequality, sexism, etc.? No, but it does mean that these
problems insofar as they are to be ministered to politically
ought to be given their proper significance. They ought to
be stripped of their quasi-religious garb, of the assumption
that their solution *equals* human salvation. They should be
placed in perspective.

Living as we do in a "mass culture" we tend to focus
upon those problems which are amenable to mass (political)
solution, and to consider them to be "the great problems of
the day." They may be that, but they are not the great
problems of the individual's day. Nor can these political so-
lutions touch in any significant way the problems which I
have *as a human being*. The "everyman" suppresses this, sub-
merges himself in the "busyness" of the everyday, and makes
certain that his life is without *essential seriousness*.

> If a man were to have his own way, he would never
> become earnest about anything; the Sophist in him
> always substitutes illusion, evasion, etc., for earnest-
> ness. [J&P, IV, p. 4311]

The everyman is immersing himself in the everyday, and in
defining himself in terms of the crowd, is guilty of the
despair of necessity. He refuses to recognize the multitude
of possibilities which his freedom offers to him. To do so
would be to live life in earnest. How much easier it is to
yield to the sophist in us, the clever coward that is our alter

ego and our temptation. Having refused to raise ourselves out of the crowd, we find it difficult to abide those who have. Having chosen to be a "nobody" we feel a certain *resentment* in the face of those who do not so choose. This resentment or envy motivates us to want to see the person who is "bigger than life," the hero or heroine, put in his place, that is, brought down to our level. The agent of this "leveling" process is, by and large, the press. We demand that the press investigate, snoop, find out all there is to know about the hero, especially if it is degrading or belittling. Then we rest easy. Cowardice, even more so than misery, loves company.

c. Talent

These considerations, true as they are, apply to "Society," and not to you. You have been able to rise above "the crowd" because you have been given something the crowd does not have. You have *talent*.

> In this case the personality is generally determined as talent, a mercantile talent, a practical talent, a mechanical talent, a mathematical talent, a poetic talent, an artistic talent, a philosophical talent. Satisfaction in life and enjoyment is sought in the development of this talent. One does not, perhaps, stop with the talent in its immediacy, one cultivates it in all ways.... [E/O, II, p. 187]

Your talent gives focus, definition, and meaning to your life; all else takes second place in both your eyes and those of the other. You can be as cruel as Lord Byron, as absent-minded as Thales stumbling into a well, as dumb as the dumbest professional athlete, it is all excused because you have talent. If talent is your life focus, then the most you could wish for is *genius*. Perhaps you have or are a genius. Perhaps your genius has even been recognized. In talking of you people mention in respectful tones, "She is a genius," and you accept the burden, always of course with suitable humility.

But genius cannot by itself elevate you out of the realm of the immediate.

> Genius is, as the word itself shows, immediateness
> (*ingenium*, that which is inborn, primitive, *primus*,
> original, *origo*, etc.), it is a natural qualification,
> genius *is born*. [GA, p. 91]

By itself your talent for mathematics, music, poetry, or ath-
letics cannot distinguish you essentially from the nightingale
which sings exceptionally well, or the jaguar which runs exceptionally fast. Your talent will distinguish you from the
crowd, only in superficial terms, in the eyes of the public
employing superficial concepts. In terms of its relation to
fate, genius is only quantitatively different from the beautiful person.

> . . . genius is constantly discovering fate, and the
> deeper the genius, the deeper he discovers it. . . . If
> he continues to be merely a genius and does not
> turn back upon himself inwardly, he will accomplish
> astounding things, and yet he will constantly suc-
> cumb before fate, if not outwardly and in a way
> which is tangible and visible to all, at least in-
> wardly. . . . If genius remains immediately deter-
> mined and turns outward, it becomes indeed great,
> and its exploits astounding, but it never comes to it-
> self, and it never becomes great in its own
> eyes. . . . The significance of genius for itself is
> null. . . . [CD, p. 89–91]

Here the point is that the truer the genius the more the
recognition both of the fact that the talent is "given" and
thus has little to do with self, and second that the talent separates one—at least superficially—from the public. What
results is an ambivalent attitude of humility and pride
toward oneself.

> It is modest of the nightingale not to require any
> one to listen to it; but it is also proud of the night-
> ingale not to care whether anyone listens to it or
> not. [GA, p. 107]

But one cannot take credit for that over which one has no
control, and so the genius can be satisfied by the products of
his talent—including the adulation of the public—only to the
extent that he can maintain to himself the "deceptive appear-
ance which suggests that the extraordinary gifts are spirit
posited by spirit" [CD, p. 885; see also J&P, I, 885]. The
extreme of the life of genius is—like the extreme of any life

—a specific madness. The madness of genius is complete absorption into fate as a kind of ironic reversal. The genius, the person capable of great feats, sees himself as driven by fate. As a result, he begins to read external circumstance as signs of fate.

> Hence a second lieutenant, if he is a genius, is able to become an emperor, to remodel the world, so that there remains only one empire and one emperor. But hence also the army may be drawn up for battle, the absolutely favorable condition may the next instant perhaps be lost, a nation of heroes may implore that the order to attack be given, but he cannot, he must wait until the fourteenth of June. And why? Because that was the date of the Battle of Marengo. [CD, p. 89][5]

Kierkegaard is here considering the life devoted to the realization of self through the development of one's talent. This person yearns to appreciate the products of her talents; and more, to hear "the others" say of her, "She is a genius." Or even more commonly, she yearns to hear of her child, "That child is a genius." Genius is talent at its best, and the life devoted to one's genius is the best that the life of talent has to offer. But this life is shipwrecked upon itself. The greater the genius, the less I can claim its products to be my own, because the greater the genius the more "inborn" are the talents. The products of this life are not *my* creations but the creations of my talent, in the same way that the obscenities of the madman are not that person's words but the products of his illness. The logic of this situation is that the genius succumb to her talent, her muse, her fate. But this is insanity. Alternatively she could claim the products as her own; accept for herself "the other's" praise. But this is only self-delusion. When the genius under consideration is that of one's child as it so often is, the problem is doubled by having the genius even one step further removed from one's self.

d. The Hedonist

But is not the point that unifocal lives, the lives of health, beauty, wealth, social place, or talent, are all a bit naive?

It *is* cute to watch a person devote his life to an idea, or a talent, and one must admire the perseverance. Artist types are often fun to have around, though on topics other than their art they can be terrible bores. Beautiful people can provide moments of diversion, but the single-mindedness of it is rather uncultured, perhaps barbarian even. It is surely unthinking. A moment's reflection teaches that "Pleasure ... is in itself a multiplicity" [E/O, p. 188]. The point then is to sample, to change ground, to leave no stone unturned; and surely to not allow the customs of society and transferred parental hang-ups to deter one's search. This life view is then single-minded in its search for pleasure but diverse in its openness to possible sources of pleasure. It is sophisticated. However, this life view is very difficult to carry through in ordinary circumstances

> ... on account of the troubles of earthly life which give man something else to think about. ... but it is not rare to see people who bungle at it a little, and when the conditions requisite for it are lacking are inclined to think that if only they had the conditions under their control they surely would have attained the happiness and joy they longed for in life. [E/O, II, p. 188]

Let us think of someone for whom all the conditions were right, who had no impediments to the satisfaction of all his desires. Think of the Emperor Nero.

> So I picture to myself the imperial voluptuary. I imagine him somewhat older, his youth is past, the light heart has escaped from him, he is already familiar with every conceivable pleasure, satiated with it. ... The immediacy of spirit is unable to break through, and yet it demands a metamorphosis, it demands a higher form of existence. But if this is to come about, an instant will arrive when the splendor of the throne, his might and power will pale, and for this he has not the courage. Then he grasps after pleasure; all the world's cleverness must devise for him new pleasures, for only in the instant of pleasure does he find repose, and when that is past he gasps with faintness. ... Then the spirit within him gathers like a dark cloud, its wrath broods over his soul, and it becomes an anguished dread which ceases not even in the moment of pleasure. ... A child who looks at him in an unaccustomed way

. . . may terrify him, it is as though this person owned him. He does not possess himself; only when the world trembles before him is he tranquilized, for then there is no one who ventures to lay hold of him.

Hence this dread of men which Nero shares with every personality of this sort. . . .

There comes a moment in a man's life when his immediacy is, as it were, ripened and the spirit demands a higher form in which it will apprehend itself as spirit. . . . now spirit would collect itself, as it were, out of this dispersion and become itself transformed. . . . if the moment is checked, if it is forced back, melancholy ensues. One may do much by way of inducing forgetfulness, one may work, one may employ other expedients more innocent than those of Nero, but melancholy remains. [E/O, II, p. 190–93]

It is no great difficulty to see why the life of diverse hedonism is unsatisfactory even on its own terms. Boredom, its ultimate enemy, is unavoidable. Satiation, depravity, and disorientation will defeat any such attempts. A life devoted to the collection of enjoyable or "interesting" experiences is an empty life. It is not a life of spirit, but one in which spirit disappears in the multitude of diversions. It is not a life in search of spirit, but rather the reverse. Nero is terrified by the glance of a child. Why is this so? Because reflected in the eyes of the child he sees not the emperor—something of which the child has no knowledge—but himself. The child "sees through" him, and in the eyes of the child he glimpses his emptiness. He is a clown who has toyed with that which was most sacred, and was given to him for his safekeeping, his own life. And what is his response to this brief glimpse of himself? It is to "induce forgetfulness" about his condition. When we think of it, we all know that those who are in a position to sample life's sweet diversions are no better off in any fundamental way than those who are not. We know that those who have thrown themselves into lives of self-indulgence are often racked with emptiness, loneliness, self-hatred, nostalgia, and yet are unwilling to change. Knowing all this, however, we would be reluctant ourselves to pass up the opportunity for such a life. Why is this so? Because we convince ourselves that we would be judicious in our use of pleasure. We would practice restraint, as if lack of restraint were what had so corrupted the spirits of all those "imperial voluptuaries." Who is deceived by such thoughts, truly deceived? The life of superficial diversions has great attraction, as does the pastry table for the child. In the latter case it is, we know, because the child is not serious about his eating habits. So it is, also, with us. The ambivalence of dread demands at one of its poles that we refuse to live *in earnest*, that we refuse to take life seriously. To throw oneself into indulgence is to say, "All I am is a potential for pleasure. The more pleasure that exists, the greater I am." No one can believe this in earnest, of course, and this is why such a life must rest upon self-deception.

e. Refined Egoism— the Aesthete

Perhaps you think that Nero was after all just a pig, a brute, a pervert. He was a vulgarian with no sense of taste or refinement. The point of life is not to enjoy drink, sex, power, cruelty, etc., but rather to enjoy one's *self*. This is a far more abstract hedonism which scoffs at the crudity of Nero's search. Of course it is not an empty self which one enjoys, but a self drinking, a self having sex, a self controlling others, etc. In this view, one's "relationships" are constituted by endless chatter about "relationships." One's sex is cluttered with endless chatter about "roles," "assertiveness," "total orgasm." Sentences not containing the words "I" and "feel" are few and far between.

Life is lived one step removed from what is "going on." This is precisely the ironic posture which Schlegel identified with freedom. At its most crude it is the dull soul for whom weekend encounter sessions have become the only form of human contact, if not entertainment; the constant blurting out of how I feel about the way you feel about me. At this level the ironic detachment which is the essence of this style has not (yet) bred cynicism. The person watches himself as he "relates" to others, but does not yet have detachment about himself *as watching*. He does not see his own ironic watching as just another of his many "roles." He still has faith. His faith is in his self, in its "growth," "openness" and its "relationships."

Think, though, of the sophisticated ironist. Of course life is to be enjoyed, but what he enjoys the most is his own superiority over life, the fact that in a sense he has risen above life. He is a cynic. And irony fully developed and yet unmastered must become cynicism because the essence of cynicism is that nothing is serious, nothing is sacred. Kierkegaard saw in this sophisticated irony the life of pleasure at its most highly developed. He also saw it in a view which had great attraction for him. He felt he had to understand it as completely as possible, what it meant *as a style of living.* This he accomplished in the first volume of *Either/Or,* his first major publication.

It was published in 1843 in two volumes of 838 pages. The structure of its pseudonymous authorship is as follows. The "editor" of *Either/Or* is Victor Eremita. He relates having purchased a secondhand desk, and in a fit of anger at not being able to open a drawer, smashes the desk, opening a secret door. Inside he finds some papers in two distinct volumes. Volume One contains the papers of A, as well as an account by A of having found a diary of one Johannes. Volume Two contains two long letters written to A by a judge known only as William.

Kierkegaard wrote Volume One of *Either/Or* during and immediately after his trip to Berlin to hear the lectures of the philosopher Schelling. These lectures, billed as the definitive refutation of Hegel, attracted some of the finest young minds in Germany. This included what remained of the Young Germans as well as the left-wing Hegelians. Frederick Engels and Arthur Schopenhauer also attended.[6] *Lucinde* and Schleiermacher's controversial defense of it had both recently been republished, creating the same scandalous reaction as they had four decades earlier. This created the model for the description of the romantic/ironic life view that is found in the first volume of *Either/Or,* both in form and in content.

In form, Volume One is an "arabesque," and as such is infinitely superior to Schlegel's *Lucinde.* It mixes genres (aphorism, essay, novel, letters); its structure is *seemingly* arbitrary; it is overtly self-conscious, making elaborate reference to its mode of publication, authorship, etc.; and its content is quasi-biographical, relating to some extent the intellectual journey of its author, as well as the affair of Regine.[7] In content it contains all of the themes of Schlegel's romanticism (irony, passivity, rebelliousness, the fragmentation of life, salvation through love, etc.). In addition, romantic personalities abound in *Either/Or*—the Wandering Jew, Don Juan, Faust, Nero, Byron, the Noble Outlaw—as do the more general themes of romanticism, the death wish, the betrayed virgin, disdain for orthodoxy and for the "herd," rejection of Hegelianism, despair as one's badge of superiority; and finally romantic character traits, melancholic, cynical, witty, introspective, sentimental, bored, resigned, skeptical, imaginative, clever, and so on. The main character of A is an attempt to distill these various and often contradictory personalities, themes, and emotions into one life view. Kierkegaard does not *describe* this view, he *shows* it through a character. As method it is artistic rather than philosophical, indirect rather than direct.

As any philosopher knows, a life view will include *at least* a metaphysics, describing in some general way the structures of existence, and as a corollary the relation between the human and nonhuman modes of existence. The latter will give an account of the uniqueness of *human* existence. All of this will have implications for one's epistemology, that is, the degrees of credibility one feels ought to be given to the various methods of understanding. And of course there will be a value theory providing a general statement of the characteristics of what is worthwhile and what is not, as well as more specifics concerning what types of people and activities are worthwhile and what types are not.

These three general elements, a metaphysics, an epistemology, and a value theory, are present in the ironic life view, although it should not be surprising that they are not systematically presented. As with all but systematic philosophers, one must dig to find them.

The metaphysics of A is one of paradox, absurdity, randomness. A does not experience his world as orderly or rational, and does not present it that way in theory.

> There seems to be something wrong with cause and effect also, that they do not rightly hang together. Tremendous and powerful causes sometimes produce small and unimpressive effects, sometimes none at all; then again it happens that a brisk little cause produces a colossal effect. [E/O, I, p. 25][8]

Paradox, not rational order, best describes the world.

> There are well known insects which die in the mo-
> ment of fecundation. So it is with all joy; life's su-
> preme and richest moment of pleasure is coupled
> with death. [E/O, I, p. 20]

And

> . . . The melancholy temperament has the greatest
> comic sense; the most exuberant is often the most
> idyllic; the debauched often the most moral; the
> doubtful often the most religious. [E/O, I, p. 20]

After describing the techniques of an arbitrary existence, A
notes "the arbitrariness in oneself corresponds to the accidental in the external world" [E/O, p. 296]. This notion of
life's structure reflecting the irrational structure of existence
is repeated by A's creation, the Seducer.

> Accursed Chance! . . . unfathomable being, barren
> mother of all . . . You whom I love with all my
> soul, in whose image I mold myself . . . I shall not
> overcome you with principles nor with what foolish
> people call character; no I will be your poet. . . .
> You who long ago must have wearied of tearing hu-
> man beings away from what they love . . . take me
> by surprise, I am ready. [I/O, I, p. 322]

This paradoxical and unpredictable nature of existence renders it futile and foolish to make great plans for oneself.

> Alas, the doors of fortune do not open inward so
> that by storming them one can force them open; but
> they open outward, and therefore nothing can be
> done. [I/O, I, p. 23]

Thus the metaphysics of randomness has led to fatalism in
practice. It has also led to skepticism in theory; such a world
could never be clearly comprehended.

> Ask me whatever questions you please, but do not
> ask me for reasons, and most often such mutually
> contradictory reasons, I generally have so many rea-
> sons, that for this reason it is impossible for me to
> give reasons. [E/O, I, p. 25]

Systematic thinkers of all kinds then are bound to fail.

> What philosophers say about reality is often as dis-
> appointing as a sign you see in a shop window,
> which reads: Pressing Done Here. If you brought

your clothes to be pressed, you would be fooled; for the sign is only for sale. [E/O, I, p. 31]

Existence is governed by chance and refuses to be neatly summarized either by the principles of empirical science or by philosophy. What distinguishes the human from the nonhuman is spirit, the power of freedom. The freedom which spirit provides is control over one's existence, but *not* in the realm of *action*. Freedom for A, who believes that the "doors of fortune do not open inward . . . and therefore nothing can be done," lies in the *imagination*. In an essay entitled "The Rotation Method" A develops what he calls the art of remembering and forgetting. It is the ability to be selective concerning what one brings in and out of consciousness, in order to control one's (experienced) world.

> Forgetting and remembering are thus identical arts, and the artistic achievement of this identity is the Archimedean point from which one lifts the whole world. [E/O, I, p. 291]

Such an artist

> . . . is in a position to play at battledore and shuttlecock with the whole of existence. The extent of one's power to forget is the final measure of one's elasticity of spirit. [E/O, I, p. 290]

For A, freedom means the ability to control the manner in which the world is experienced, which for A is equivalent to controlling "the whole of existence." This type of control is appropriate to the ironist, for whom "everything is light, beautiful, transitory." It is a control which bandies existence about, plays at badminton with existence. It is *reflective* control, not the control of the man of affairs. The busy, successful bourgeois is lacking in spirit, lacking in what distinguishes the human.

> . . . every human being who lacks a sense for idleness proves that his consciousness has not been elevated to the level of the humane. There is a restless activity which excludes a man from the world of the spirit, setting him in a class with the brutes, whose instincts impel them always to be on the move. [E/O, I, p. 285][9]

In exercising the freedom of poetic memory the ironist

is creating a thing of beauty of his own life. He is justified in being what "foolish men of character" would consider fast and loose with reality because beauty is after all a "sentimental theme in fantastic form." This demands that feeling, knowledge, and will remain free and spontaneous, free of both stylistic and ontological restraint. Kierkegaard refers to A as an "aesthete" not as some say because he is concerned with *feeling* but rather because the artistic process (as romantically understood) provides A with his life model. Reality is amorphous, unstructured, and random, as is the medium of an art work. Freedom is ideally the control of an artist over his medium. The paradigmatic knower is not the mathematician, the scientist, or the philosopher. It is the poet, for whom existence is an inexhaustible source of possible arrangements.

This metaphysics has implications for a theory of value. Existence as so described is not a system of Aristotelian final causes, of "immanent teleologies." Nor is there room for a doctrine of salvation in the Christian mold. No concepts of earthly vocations or divine reunion can constitute the ultimate good for man. For A "it is the end and aim of every man to enjoy himself" [E/O, I, p. 285]. The ultimate evil is then enjoyment's opposite, boredom; not pain, of course, since that can and often should be enjoyed. The metaphysics of a life view must be such as to account for the possibility of evil, i.e., solve the problem of evil. For A,

> Boredom depends on the nothingness which pervades reality; it causes dizziness like that produced by looking down a yawning chasm, and this dizziness is infinite. [E/O, I, p. 287]

The point here is that every life view contains an idea about what the best is that life has to offer. It will also contain an idea of how it is that humans specifically fail, that is, what is evil for a human being. The deeper and more profound a life view, the deeper and more profound will be human evil. For the aesthete, human evil equals boredom, just as for the Countess it equaled loss of physical beauty.

What, then, is it which most generally extinguishes boredom? Not pleasure, of course, since pleasure can be and often is boring. It is the "interesting." But this can be achieved in a mature sense only once one has despaired; despaired of the possibility of earthly salvation through action. We have already seen that "Of all the ridiculous things, it seems to me the most ridiculous is to be a busy man of affairs." And so,

> It is impossible to live artistically before one has made up one's mind to abandon hope. . . . Hope was one of the dubious gifts of Prometheus; instead of giving men foreknowledge of the immortals, he gave them hope. [E/O, I, p. 288]

Having despaired, one can practice the "principle of limitation" which is "the only saving principle in the world." It advocates the use of self-discipline and poetic memory to create singularly *intensive* experiences. This practice distinguishes the artist from the bungler, Johannes the Seducer from Don Juan, the aesthetes from the men of affairs who are always so busy and

> are precisely on this account the most tiresome. . . . this species of animal life . . . like all lower forms of life . . . is marked by a high degree of fertility, and multiplies endlessly. [E/O, I, p. 284]

Keeping busy, changing diversions, looking always for new and different and more lasting pleasures is the *extensive* method, the method of Nero. It is doomed to failure, unable to escape boredom. It "needs to be supported by illusion." Thus one must face reality, be "transparent to oneself" and despair of the extensive method.

The last section of Volume One is the 144-page "Diary of the Seducer." It is the story in diary form of Johannes' first acquaintance with the young Cordelia, of the artful and unscrupulous manner in which he introduces himself into her life and then her affection, and finally of her seduction. It is a consciously worked out and intricately planned seduction taking several months, and ending on the night of its culmination.

Johannes one day spies the ankle of a young girl as she descends from a carriage. He decides at this instant that he must possess her, a possession which in his mind takes the form of sexual seduction. Think for a minute of the continuum of: rape, seduction, mutually consenting sex. Rape results only in a brief physical possession. Though it is a terrible violation, the rapist does not possess the *person*, only the body and only briefly. Mutually consenting sex involves either no possession (if frivolous) or mutual possession (if serious).

> Mere possession is not worth much, and the means which such lovers employ are generally wretched enough. They do not disdain the use of money, power, influence, soporifics, and so on. But what enjoyment can there be in love if there is not the most absolute self-surrender, at least on one side? But such submission as a rule requires spirit, and such lovers are usually destitute of spirit. [E/O, I, p. 331]

Seduction is the process by which one is induced through subterfuge into willing to be possessed, while the seducer remains unpossessed and in control. In this sense it is, as only Kierkegaard saw, the most natural relationship for an ironist, for it is the essence of the ironist's posture that he stand outside of himself and remain uncommitted. If it is possession and control one wants, seduction (whether sexual or not) is what is called for. Seduction *is* ironic love.

Johannes realizes that in her present youthful state his victim, Cordelia, is not "mature" enough to give herself completely to him. He must educate her in life, tense the string of the bow, as he says. This takes the form of arranging for her engagement to another, instilling in her a cynicism for the courtship ritual, inducing her to break her engagement to the other and accept his own proposal, and then manipulating the relationship so that it seems to her that she has broken it off. She is not sure, but in any case she is heartbroken. A friend's country cottage is provided for her lonely mourning. On the first night Johannes appears at the door, and the plan of several months is culminated. She never sees him again.

Of the Seducer, A says,

> His life had been an attempt to realize the task of living poetically. With a keenly developed talent for discerning the interesting in life, he constantly reproduced the experience more or less poetically. His Diary is therefore neither historically exact nor simple fiction, not indicative but subjunctive. [E/O, I, p. 300]

Johannes has, according to A, a

> ... poetic temperament which, we might say, is not

rich enough, or, perhaps not poor enough, to distinguish poetry and reality from one another. [E/O, I, p. 301]

Kierkegaard was at his most brilliant in the manner in which he introduces the Seducer. In the essay immediately before the Diary he introduces clearly the concepts of poetic memory, the principle of limitation and the "interesting." We chuckle when A advises against marriage, friendship, and vocation as destructive of the interesting. And we laugh heartily when he exhibits the life of the interesting by telling us of an interesting man.

At every opportunity he was ready with a little philosophical lecture, a very tiresome harangue. Almost in despair, I suddenly discovered that he perspired copiously when talking. I saw the pearls of sweat gather on his brow, unite to form a stream, glide down his nose, and hang at the extreme point of his nose in a drop-shaped body. From the moment of making this discovery, all was changed. I even took pleasure in inciting him to begin his philosophical instruction, merely to observe the perspiration on his brow and at the tip of his nose. [E/O, I, p. 295]

We are in a light and humorous frame of mind in receiving these romantic instructions in the art of living. What harm could come of pursuing the life of the interesting with these tools? But then Johannes enters the scene; a vicious, psychopathic personality not only devoid of conscience but ready to ruthlessly exploit anyone in search of the interesting. And what greater symbol of exploitation in the nineteenth century than sexual seduction? Much as the early 1960s were "seduced" by the light, friendly, do-your-own-thing life view of the "flower child" only to be informed of its possibilities by Charles Manson, so the reader is seduced by the romantic wit into believing it harmless and charming. The Seducer jolts one back to reality. The relationship between Julius and Lucinde had been extolled as the ideal of romantic love. Schlegel had consciously established it as an alternative to the bourgeois ideal. The latter had claimed that a man needed three distinct relationships which could not overlap in the same woman. He needed a wife for bearing and raising children as well as to manage the household. He needed a mistress for the obvious reasons, and an *âme soeur* with whom he could discuss intellectual and personal themes.

Julius and Lucinde challenged the claim that one relationship could not be all three. It was the ideal romantic relationship, or so it was thought. In the life philosophy of A there was no principle which suggested that one ought respect the other person. Where Schlegel had recommended that the person be able to tune himself, there was nothing in his views to restrict one from "tuning" another. Johannes says,

> Like an archer, I release the string, tighten it again, listen to its song, my battle ode. . . .
>
> She must be developed inwardly, she must feel an elasticity of soul, she must learn to evaluate the world. [E/O, I, p. 345, p. 356]

All this must take place before the climactic act, and so Johannes prepares Cordelia as one would marinate a steak.

Hegel had suggested that a life based upon individual inclination would by some necessity lead to perversion. Kierkegaard's point in separating Johannes and A is to show only that Johannes' life is a consistent (though not a necessary) application of the life view of romanticism. But it is in a way more consistent than the relationship of Julius to Lucinde. For why should Julius, who admittedly despised all restriction, remain restricted by a respect for the rights of Lucinde? Isn't it true then that Kierkegaard has provided a new ideal of romantic love, the love of Johannes for Cordelia?

Our point must be then that the life of self-centered hedonism whether it be the simpleminded Countess or the equally simpleminded hippy, whether it be the brutish vulgarianism of Nero or the refined aestheticism of A, contains within it the possibility of the most sadistic exploitive behavior. It contains that possibility in the sense that the view contains no principles which rule it out.

Because the life of the aesthete lacks seriousness, he tries on life-styles, whole personalities, as one would try on clothes in a store, and watches himself all the while. Eventually he must become cynical about himself, about his search. To advice that he change his ways, he responds,

> Yes, I perceive perfectly that there are two possibilities, one can either do this or that. My sincere opinion . . . is as follows: Do it/or don't do it—you will regret both. [E/O, II, p. 163]

The Judge is right when he says to the aesthete,

> . . . Life is a masquerade, you explain, and for you
> this is inexhaustible material for amusement; and so
> far, no one has succeeded in knowing you; for every
> revelation you make is always an illusion. . . . In
> fact you are nothing; you are merely a relation to
> others. . . . [E/O, II, p. 163]

The refined egoist masquerades as a self-searcher, but in fact
is engaged in a most clever program of self-obscurity, remaining obscure to himself and to others. He is shrewd,
clever, witty, insightful, disarming, and scared. This style
also has its specific madness. Judge William notes,

> I have seen men who played hide and seek so long
> that at last madness through them obtruded disgust-
> ingly upon others their secret thoughts. . . . can you
> think of anything more frightful than that it might
> end with your nature being resolved into a multi-
> plicity, that you really might become many, become,
> like those unhappy demonics, a legion, and you thus
> would have lost the inmost and holiest thing of all
> in a man, the unifying power of personality? [E/O,
> II, p. 163]

But in the range of everyday pathology, he experiments
with himself.

> If the despairing self is active, it really is related to
> itself only as experimenting. . . . in the last resort it
> lacks seriousness and is able only to conjure up a
> show of seriousness when the self bestows upon its
> experiments its utmost attention. [SUD, p. 202]

There is something which he knows he must relinquish, but
cannot. He is carrying a secret, which he cannot reveal,
which is that he cannot be everything to himself. Defiantly
he tries to satisfy himself with himself, to rule over his life, but

> . . . this ruler is a king without a country, he rules
> really nothing; his condition, his dominion is subject
> to the dialectic that every instant revolution is legiti-
> mate. [SUD, p. 203]

Revolution is legitimate because when he "changes selves" he
is not breaking with anything which could be called "himself." This is the despair of possibility referred to earlier.

The self becomes an abstract possibility which tries

itself out with floundering in the possible, but does not budge from the spot. . . . To become is a movement from the spot, but to become oneself is a movement at the spot. [SUD, p. 169]

This state Kierkegaard calls variously "shut-upness," "the demonical," "introversion," "the despair of defiance," "dread of the good." It is the most volatile, explosive, and dangerous form of despair, and the closest to madness. Yet in our time it is so common.

Ernest Wolf points out, for example, that the practicing therapist finds very little of the typical neuroses of Freud's day—hysteria, hand-washing compulsion, phobias, etc. Rather the patients, affluent urbanites, exhibit the less specific symptoms of depression, disintegrating marriages, incapacitating work inhibitions, hypochondriacal preoccupations, frenzied searches, perversion, and so forth.[10]

Kernberg focuses upon the category of narcissism as a prevalent contemporary pathology. He describes narcissistic personalities as exhibiting

> . . . excessive self-absorption usually coinciding with a superficially smooth and effective social adaption, but with serious distortions in their internal relationships with other people. They present various combinations of intense ambitiousness, grandiose fantasies, feelings of inferiority, and other dependence on external admiration and acclaim. Along with feelings of emptiness and continuous search for gratification, of strivings for brilliance, wealth, power and beauty, there are serious deficiencies in their capacity to love and to be concerned about others. . . . Chronic uncertainty and dissatisfaction about themselves, conscious or unconscious exploitiveness and ruthlessness toward others are also characteristics. . . .[11]

I include these references to modern psychologists not with the idea that concepts such as narcissism can clarify in any way Kierkegaard's analysis. It is, if anything, the other way around. They are cited to draw the relationship between what Kierkegaard describes under the broad heading of "aesthetic life" and the language of our therapeutic age. The differences between Kierkegaard's approach to this life view and that of the therapist are immense, and will be discussed. For now I would like to summarize the foregoing by focusing in upon the concepts and experiences of guilt and of time, and how they function in the aesthetic life.

Guilt

First, none of the five styles of life discussed so far employ any concept of sin or actual moral guilt. Let us not be confused about what is at issue here. We can distinguish clearly between guilt feelings and actual guilt. Within the idea of actual guilt we must distinguish moral from legal guilt. If a drunkard wakes up *falsely* believing that he killed a child in a hit-and-run accident, he may "feel guilty," he may believe that he is morally guilty and/or that he is legally guilty. On the other hand, if he had done it but does not remember, he would *be* morally guilty and *be* legally guilty, but not *feel* any guilt. The point is that all three concepts are distinct, and none implies the others.

The aesthete understands the concept of actual legal guilt, and employs it in his own life. It is a matter of prudence that he do so. He understands something about the concept of moral guilt, the fact that others employ the concept in their own lives, and the fact that others will use the concept to judge him. Actual moral guilt concerns the aesthete only in his concern over how others view him. But this is *shame* and not guilt, or even guilt feelings. Shame is the anxiety of not having lived up to the moral expectations of others. Guilt feeling is the anxiety of not having lived up to one's own moral expectations of oneself. Thus the aesthete employs in his own life the concepts of legal guilt and shame, but never employs the concepts of actual guilt and thus never has guilt feelings. In this respect the aesthete is oddly both an ancient and a modern. He is an ancient in that it is often said of the classical Greeks that their societies were founded upon shame, and had no concept of guilt. This received its philosophic expression in Socrates' claim that no person could knowingly do evil. Immorality is always a direct consequence of ignorance. And since man is not responsible for his ignorance, he is not responsible for his immorality. We have seen already that Kierkegaard considered the Judeo-Christian tradition to have transcended this concept of evil, and thus introduced the concept of sin.

And Kirkegaard himself had advanced tremendously the theoretical understanding of the possibility of knowingly doing evil with his concepts of dread, the self, and especially self-deception. With the latter concept, Kierkegaard can say that sin does indeed derive from ignorance, but it is *willed* ignorance.

The aesthete is also very modern, for it is a characteristic of our age that the ideas of sin and of actual moral guilt have been destroyed. Of course our age retains the idea of legal guilt. But

> . . . the man who merely by finiteness learns to recognize his guilt is lost in finiteness and in the end the question whether one is guilty or not cannot be decided except by external, judicial, exceedingly imperfect way. . . . He . . . never really comprehends that he is guilty. [CD, p. 144]

As Thomas Szaz says,

> Punishment is no longer fashionable. Why? Because—with its corollary, reward—it makes some people guilty and others innocent, some good and others evil; in short, it creates moral distinctions among men, and to the "democratic" mentality this is odious. Our age seems to prefer a meaningless collective guilt to a meaningful individual responsibility.[12]

The point Kierkegaard made in *Two Ages* about the homogenizing of modern life here merges with the discussion of moral guilt. And the latter merges with the question of legal guilt. The present age does not believe in retribution because it will not accept moral guilt. The latter concept offends us because it creates *radical* distinctions between people. The present age prefers the therapeutic approach. All people are radically (at bottom) the same, only "the environment" creates (artificial) differences. A therapeutic age pretends to explain all aspects of human life within naturalistic categories, where the prime example of the latter is physics. Kierkegaard realized that an attempt to do this would destroy the concept of guilt (sin).

> . . . as soon as sin is talked about as a sickness, an abnormality, a poison, a disharmony, then the concept too is falsified. [CD, p. 14]

Thus when the sciences (sociology, psychology, social psychology) interpret the human person in purely naturalistic terms the concepts of sin and guilt are destroyed, but so also is the concept of the individual person. How does one explain the juvenile delinquent?

> The child is represented as a regular little angel, but the depraved environment cast it into perdition. . . . Or the child is represented as so fundamentally wicked that good example can do it no good. . . . Or the child was, as most children are, neither good nor bad, but then fell into good company and became good, or into bad company and became bad. But the middle term! . . . If one has not the middle terms at hand promptly and clearly, then the concepts of original sin, of sin, of the race, of the individual, are lost, and the child along with them. [CD, p. 68]

By "the middle term" here Kierkegaard means the self, a relation which relates itself to itself. Sin, guilt, is a consequence of the self, that is of the person himself, not his "nature," his upbringing, his instincts, his social pressures, or his peer group. Any other attempt to explain human behavior loses the human in the process.

Nowadays guilt is "treated" as a problem. The problem is (nowadays) that people *feel* guilty. The solution is construed simply as removing the feeling of guilt. But this confuses guilt and shame (the superego is after all constituted by social and parental expectations), and more important it ignores the question of whether the person *is* guilty. To be guilty is to be *in debt*. It is to *owe* something. There is therefore a demand that the debt be paid, and when it is, the guilt is removed. It is not sufficient to assume this view of having an "eye for an eye" quality about it, as if *that* constituted a refutation. The "eye for an eye" slogan is just that; and when interpreted subtly, generates a perfectly respectable retributionist theory of justice and punishment.[14] The therapist will say nowadays that it is not his job to be concerned with actual guilt, that is the cleric's domain. This may be true, but neither then would it be his job to convince the patient (his client) that all feelings of guilt are unjustified, nor then could he claim to be able to set right (cure) the entire individual, which (excepting the bodily) is his implicit claim. Thus the discussion of guilt has brought us to the borders of psychology as an account of human action and healer of the human spirit.

Judge William recognizes that the absence of any concept of actual moral guilt, of moral goodness and evil, is essential to A's life view.[15] Thus when he places the choice before A, he says, "My either/or does not in the first instance denote the choice between good and evil; it denotes the choice whereby one chooses good and evil/or excludes them." [E/O, II, p. 173]

Time

The second characteristic of the aesthetic life is its peculiar way of experiencing time. That the experience of time is essential and peculiar to true human living has been commonplace at least since Rousseau. Animals do not experience themselves as *in time* and thus have no history *for themselves*. Human life is not a summary of moments. A biographer does not divide the subject's life into equal temporal segments and proceed to describe them in order. A human life is an organized system of (overlapping) projects, some instantaneous, others lifelong. Time is experienced within human living as past, present, future relative to these projects. Kierkegaard's thesis is that the aesthete cannot make sense of time, cannot relate to past, present, and future. The result is that the aesthete is forced to "live" in one of them while trying (self-deceptively) to ignore the other two.

Of course it is not in practice possible to live only in the present and still function in an ordinary (noninstitutionalized) environment. Theoretically, though, it is conceivable, and this possibility Kierkegaard sees represented by the mythic character of Don Juan, especially as portrayed in Mozart's *Don Giovanni*. Don Juan *merely wanders*. When a woman (any woman) appears, she virtually falls into his arms.

> Only in this manner can Don Juan become epic, in that he constantly finishes, and constantly begins again from the beginning, for his life is the sum of repellent moments which have no coherence, his life as moment is the sum of the moments, as the sum of the moments is the moment. [E/O, I, p. 95]

Of course even if one's life focus is sexual, others do not "fall into one's arms." A little planning is generally necessary, and this means a more or less active consideration of the future. This shows that an attempt to live in the present, so far as it is successful, is an attempt to live a passive existence. A passive existence is spiritless; it is to immerse oneself in the finite; and it is to attempt to rid oneself of the past and of the future. To plan is not only to *consider* the future and thus transcend the present, it is also to *commit oneself* to a project. The latter entails self-restraint, that is, spirited control of one's self. Thus the concepts of living for the present, denial of past, the praise of passivity, the avoidance of commitments, and lack of faith in the future are all intertwined. All of these elements are found explicitly in A. These elements are found also in the "consciousness movement" of the late twentieth century. One of the early and more respectable ideologues of the movement, Fritz Perls, states, "The past is no more and the future is not yet. Only the now exists."[16] In this context serious human commitments (wife, husband, parent, friend, teacher, etc.) are *at best* relegated to the status of "social roles" and "peer binding" and at worst have their foundation in "inhibitions" or "repressions." That this emphasis upon the present, and its correlate, the inability to establish committed relationships, evinces fatalism, that is, a lack of confidence in the future, was noted by Christopher Lasch.

> . . . the fear and rejection of parenthood . . . the perception of marriage as merely one in a series of nonbinding commitments, reflects a growing distrust of the future and a reluctance to make provisions for it. . . . The cult of interpersonal relations represents the final dissolution of bourgeois optimism and self-confidence.[17]

So it is with A, who finds, "Of all the ridiculous things, it seems to me the most ridiculous is to be a busy man of affairs," and also finds, "Time flows, life is a stream, people say, and so on. I do not notice it. Time stands still, and I with it," and finally, "the doors of fortune do not open inward . . . therefore nothing can be done" [E/O, I, pp. 23, 24, 25].

But the more reflective aesthete escapes the present and lodges himself firmly in the future. Here we have the Don Juan at the other end of the aesthetic spectrum, Johannes the Seducer. Don Juan was not chasing women, he was passive, was being chased. Johannes is related to the future. He chases women, or more exactly, he chases after the "perfect moment."[18] Judge William is keenly aware of this, and of the fact that only in this trivial sense can the aesthete be said to be a "man of faith." He quotes the aesthete.

> What! Am I supposed not to have faith? Why I believe that in the inmost depths of the stillness of the forest, where the trees are reflected in the dark water, in its mysterious darkness . . . there lives a being, a nymph, a maiden; I believe she is more beautiful than any one can conceive . . . I believe that I should be happy, the only man deserving to be so called, if I could catch her and possess her; I believe that in my soul there is a longing to search the whole world, I believe that I would be happy if that longing were satisfied. . . . do not say, then, that I am not strong in faith and fervent in spirit. [E/O, II, p. 204]

The language reminds one of Hyperion's, who found in the beautiful young Diotima his goddess of love. The experience is of having "returned," returned to a state of innocence, harmony, and simplicity. If we recall Kierkegaard's description of the origin of the self, this would be a return to the state prior to the first realization of possibility, prior to freedom, to the awareness of time, and prior to dread. In such a state existential anxiety does not exist precisely because the self does not exist. John Lilly found Nirvana in Arica Training which made him feel

> . . . just completely pure; like a baby in the womb. Totally without deviation or sin; no responsibilities and yet responsible for everybody. . . . No contradictions; in total tune with the universe. I had never known what that meant before, being right in tune with matter—with the cosmos and nature, with other people . . . everything.[19]

Thus finding oneself in this context, one which constitutes the prime spiritualism of the late twentieth century, means finding an experience which brings one back to the pre-self. Insofar as the reflective aesthete is future-oriented, insofar as he searches, plans, etc., it is ultimately to accomplish a *return* and not a development. The aesthetic life's relation to time, then, is an attempt to plan the future in such a way that the past of the pre-self will be revived. When that occurs the person will "live in the present," that is, will become passive, innocent, undivided, unified with nature, and nonhuman.

This discussion brings us back to one of the central questions of romanticism. Is it possible for a person to "return" to a state more simple, innocent, and anxiety-free? From the very beginning with Rousseau the tendency among romantic theorists was to mourn the loss of innocence but insist that the past cannot be recaptured *in the same form*. What was lost must be reattained in a manner consistent with man's new existence as a free, knowing being. This is nothing other than the dialectic. Each individual breaks from the innocent ignorance of childhood into a state of free anxious isolation. He cannot return but must press ahead to a new higher integration. While this was the theory underlying romanticism, Kierkegaard noted that the practicing aesthete had not learned the lesson. There are those who live in "hope"; who merely dream about the past. There are those who practice "recollection"; who actively attempt to bring back the past as it was. There are those, finally, who practice "repetition"; who attempt to regain an integrity that was lost but in a manner that does not relinquish what has been gained. To practice repetition requires insight into just what human integrity is, what a person is, and what is demanded of a person. Without this it is not possible to know what one cannot give up in the drive toward human integrity. But you will have guessed, I am certain, that this insight is not enough to bring one to repetition.

> He who would only hope is cowardly, he who would only recollect is a voluptuary, but he who wills repetition is a man, and the more expressly he knows how to make his purpose clear, the deeper he is a man. [R, p. 34]

In his short work *Repetition* Kierkegaard tells the story of a man, Constantine Constantius, who attempts an elaborate recollection and fails. He realizes the necessity of failure and yet is not able to will the necessary move. He is also not able to help a young friend whom he understands to have the same problem.

> Repetition is too transcendent for me also. I can circumnavigate myself, but I cannot erect myself above

myself, I cannot find the Archimedean point. [R, p. 90]

It takes courage to press one's life forward, to use the temporal in oneself to achieve the eternal. How much easier it is to pretend to oneself that there is nothing to gain in pressing one's self forward.

> To despair over oneself, in despair to will to be rid of oneself, is the formula for all despair. . . . [SUD, p. 153]

What is accomplished in this case is at best a life which is segmented into temporary experiences of return (unitive consciousness, peak experiences, bliss, ultimate states, oneness, cosmic awareness, cosmic play, individual synergy, etc.). These segments constitute a temporary killing of time. Time is the enemy of the aesthete. It separates the reflective dreaming aesthete from his goal. It destroys with its inexorable movement the attempt of the immediate aesthete to live in the present, and likewise it overcomes the reflective aesthete's attempts to rid himself of himself. The occupation of the aesthete is, in attempting to be rid of himself, to "kill time."

> That time (succession, one after the other) is or can be man's worst enemy is curiously expressed in many suggestive turns of speech: To kill time, to slay time—and conversely, that time drags out in a *deadly* way. [J&P, IV, p. 4792]

This ends for now our discussion of the style of living of individual self-realization in one dimension. There is no claim by Kierkegaard to have "proven" it to be inadequate. Its inadequacy can only be established as the result of a *choice* by you in your own life. Kierkegaard's aim is only to exhibit its features, and this is done *in his works* with brilliant clarity.

SEVEN

THE GROUP—
IN ONE DIMENSION

T he life of the aesthete (the ironist, the romantic) represented to Kierkegaard the best of what the life of one-dimensional individual self-realization had to offer. It is for this reason that he devoted such a large portion of his early work to it. Kierkegaard was not interested in superficial criticisms of a life view or of criticisms of its perverted forms. This would be cheap and dishonest. Rather, he takes a view and formulates it in its ideal form, evaluating the best it has to offer. This is what Volume One of *Either/Or* did for the life view in question.

Volume Two does the same for the life of bourgeois virtue. In his short work *Two Ages* Kierkegaard described and criticized the actually existing forms of bourgeois life. It pointed to the fact that bourgeois life *in practice* was nothing more than a self-indulgent and cowardly form of despair—the despair of finitude and necessity. But as a criticism of the bourgeois life view—the life of fulfillment through commitment to others—this is inadequate. A detailed and successful criticism of Stalinist Russia, for example, is only that. It is not also a criticism of Marxism unless it is accompanied by an argument to the effect that the latter leads inevitably to the former. Kierkegaard knew that a criticism of bourgeois life had to be directed at the best it had to offer, and he did this in Volume Two of *Either/Or*. The life of bourgeois virtue, of self-realization through commitment to others, Kierkegaard calls the *ethical life view.*

Kierkegaard learned much from Hegel. One of Hegel's

121

insights was to contrapose the life views of individual sentiment with that of social custom *(Sittlichkeit)*. To live the
ideal life of customary morality means more than anything
else to make commitments. To be a *member* of society
rather than an ironic observer is to be a friend, a spouse, a
parent, and it is to take one's place in the economic sphere
according to one's vocation. It is to take all of these relationships seriously, enter into them openly, and keep one's commitments faithfully. Judge William is such a man. Of
himself he notes,

> I sacrifice myself for my profession, my wife, my
> children, or, more properly expressed, I do not sacri-
> fice myself for them, but I find in them my satisfac-
> tion and joy. [E/O, II, p. 174]

Here the Judge has put his finger on what seems on the surface to be a contradiction in the idea of *self*-fulfillment
through commitment to others. Doesn't a person have to
make a choice: I look out for me (for "number one") or for
others? If I look out for others, must I not sacrifice at least
some of my own needs? The Judge has read Hegel. He
knows that what *seems* to be a conflict can be "mediated"
into a higher synthesis. The harmonious synthesis of self-in-
terest and social commitment is self-fulfillment *through* service to others. No conflict need exist.

The Judge is a successful man of affairs, backbone of
the community, defender of orthodoxy, of marriage, friendship, hard work, and self-sacrifice. He is a true hero who is
destined to reside eventually in the annals of bourgeois
saints. The point is that if there is something fundamentally
wrong with the Judge's life view, then bourgeois life is rot-
ten at its core.

The life view of the Judge is more easily discerned than
that of A, because he is a more orderly person and thus a
more systematic thinker than A. What is more, he writes
very long letters. Compared to A the Judge is, in the most
general sense, a rationalist. Existence is, with the one exception of individual human action, governed by rigid necessity.
To understand this necessity philosophy, not poetry, is appropriate.

> The spheres with which philosophy properly deals,
> which properly are the spheres of thought are logic,
> nature and history. Here necessity rules. . . . [E/O,
> II, p. 178]

Poetry and art "provide only an imperfect reconciliation with life . . . when you fix your gaze upon poetry and art you are not beholding reality" [E/O, II, p. 277]. All areas except individual choice are law-governed and predictable. In these areas certainty can be achieved. "In the act of thinking, my relation to the thing thought is one of necessity" [E/O, II, p. 277]. In fact the Judge claims, "The absolute *is* for the fact that I think it"; but this does not mean that I am free to think whatever I want and expect it to be true since "my thinking of the absolute is the self-thinking of the absolute in me" [E/O, II, p. 220]. This is, of course, pure Hegelianism—jargon and all. The only exception to this rigid necessity is the distinction between good and evil, which can never be either discovered or created by thinking, but only by will or freedom. Freedom is for Judge William the individuating characteristic of the human person, as it is for the aesthete. Spirit is the power of human freedom, but for the Judge it is precisely this which the aesthete lacks; "within the aesthetic domain . . . spirit is not determined as spirit, but is immediately determined" [E/O, II, p. 185].

What kind of freedom does spirit bring? Not the aesthete's freedom to imaginatively construct existence as one will; rather it is the freedom to choose one's self. But the concept of self-choice takes on meaning only within the framework of Judge William's metaphysics which contains

> The ethical thesis that every man has a calling . . . [which] is the expression for the fact that there is a rational ordering of things in which every man, if he will, fills his place in such a way that he expresses at once the universal—human and the individual. [E/O, II, p. 297]

Put in another way,

> The individual has his teleology in himself. . . . His self is the goal toward which he strives. . . . [However] In the movement toward himself the individual cannot relate himself negatively toward his environment. . . . His self must be open in due relation to his entire concretion. [E/O, II, p. 279]

To choose oneself does not then mean to *create* oneself. This is the view referred to as the despair of defiance. It means rather to commit oneself to becoming the person which the "rational ordering of things" has determined that one should be. Self-choice means self-acceptance; the accept-ance of, in Homeric Greek terms, one's *moira*. The Judge is aware of the relation between his idea of self-choice and the Greek concept of *moira* (natural place, fate, destiny).

> There is a category which means "to choose one-self," a somewhat modernized Greek category; it is my favorite category and applies to the individual life as a whole. . . . [SLW, p. 124]

It is a "modernized" version because for the Greeks whether or not one lived one's *moira* was a matter of whether or not one had self-knowledge. Thus we have Socrates' idea—which was also Homer's—that knowledge leads automatically to vir-tue, to "taking one's place." The Judge is committed rather to the Judeo-Christian conception that virtue (or sin) is a matter of *willing* and not (only) of knowing. It is up to the individual to decide not what his place is in the rational or-der but whether or not he will take his place. If he accepts his place his life task is just beginning, namely to *develop* this ethically planned self.

> The aim of his activity is himself, but not as arbi-trarily determined, for he has himself as a task which is set for him . . . a concrete self which stands in reciprocal relations with his surroundings, these conditions of life, this natural order. This self which is the aim is not merely a personal self but a social, a civic self. [E/O, II, p. 267]

Thus man's freedom, that which distinguishes him from all else, lies not in deciding who he is to be, or in creating a place for himself in existence, it lies rather in the ability to accept (or not) one's place, and carry out (or not) the duties assigned to it. This resolves the seeming split between the human (freedom) and the natural (necessity). Man is part of the natural scheme, he has a necessity, but he is free to accept or reject it. He is free to be virtuous or be a sinner. This resolves also the split between duty and inclination. For if one's acceptance is true, the duties will appear not as ex-ternal prohibitions, but as flowing directly from one's per-sonality. One is being required, after all, to choose that for which one is best suited. There will be a mediated harmony between the universal (duty connected with one's place as determined by the natural order) and the particular (the natural inclinations of the person as an individual). The

Judge himself has achieved this mediation, which is why he is able, as we saw, to receive personal fulfillment through self-sacrifice, to effect self-development through self-denial.

Before one is able to choose oneself, it is necessary to despair, to choose despair. This is the active choice to give up hope in the aesthetic life, the life of defiance, of attempted self-creation, the life of flight from one's self. To will despair is to stop running from one's self, one's place, one's task. It is *resignation.*

> Here again is manifest the importance of willing one's despair, of willing in an infinite sense, in an absolute sense, for such willing is identical with absolute resignation. [E/O, II, p. 225]

This requires courage. But there is help, an aid to the requisite courage, for at the moment of self-choice "he is most thoroughly absorbed in the root by which he is connected with the whole" [E/O, II, p. 220][1] Having despaired, courageously resigned himself, ended his life of defiance (Greek: *hybris),* his life can be transformed into a work of art, a thing of beauty. For if, as Kant says, the work of art displays purposiveness without purpose, is the result of rule-governed activity freely chosen for its own sake, then the man who has freely chosen to develop his "ethically planned" *telos* creates a work of art of his life. His life

> ... is a work of freedom, but at the same time it is immanent teleology, and hence it is here only that there can be any question of beauty. [E/O, II, p. 279]

Suppose we try to bring this discussion down to earth. Think for a minute that you have a child, in his early twenties, brilliant, talented, and well educated. As far as you can determine he supports himself on unemployment, sleeps during the day, drinks and socializes at night. You decide that the time has come to have a talk. But what will you argue? That he is wasting his life, of course; that he is throwing away his talents, his education; that he is being irresponsible. Your hope for him is that instead he find a job that coincides with his talents, get married, join a church, have children, stop living only for himself, stop running from whatever it is that scares him. You want him to become a responsible person. What does your argument assume? It assumes that your child has responsibilities by virtue of his talents and education; that there is a place for him in the social order; that he has an obligation to take this place; that despite what he believes he will be more contented having taken his place; that his life of self-indulgence is a form of escape; that he should resign himself to his obligations. That this is his choice, but he is responsible no matter which way he chooses. What your argument presupposes is the life view which the Judge has articulated.

Let us now contrapose the two life views each from its own perspective.

For A, existence is random, unpredictable, amorphous. Man's ability to comprehend it according to traditional epistemological models is exceedingly limited. It is the imaginative construction of the poet, not the rational discourse of the philosopher, which supplies the ideal of the knower. And it is this power of imaginative construction which provides for freedom, the elasticity of spirit which separates out the human. The bourgeois lacks this, lacks spirit, and is thus pre-human. The purpose of life is to escape from the greatest of all evils, boredom. The fool attempts this through "busyness" (business) and diversion. The aesthete has the self-knowledge to recognize boredom, the courage to despair, the craft to practice poetic memory, and the self-discipline to implement the principle of limitation. In this way, the aesthete creates a work of beauty of his own existence, and is saved.

For Judge William, existence is orderly and (with one exception) predictable. Man's ability to comprehend it with clarity and certainty is secure. Science and philosophy provide the models of ideal knowledge in all but the realm of human freedom. Poetry provides only illusion. It is this freedom of (self-) choice, elasticity of spirit, which separates out the human. The aesthete has not chosen himself, thus has no spirit, and thus is pre-human. The greatest good is to become oneself, to freely accept necessity. This takes concrete form in the exercise of the "civic virtues" of marriage, friendship, and vocation. The greatest evil is defiance, the cowardly act of refusing to choose oneself. The ethicist has the self-knowledge to recognize this place, the courage to despair, and the self-discipline to live out his immanent teleology. In this way the ethicist creates a work of art out of his own existence, and is saved.

With the exception of the short concluding sermon of the "Jutland Priest," to be discussed later, *Either/Or* ends at this point. That is, it contains a presentation of two complete life views with no judgment as to which is to be preferred. In fact, as has been noted, Kierkegaard rejects both life views in favor of a third. It must be emphasized that there is no decisive judgment in *Either/Or;* or any statements which could be said to be Kierkegaard's views, as to whether one or the other life view is superior. The Judge has criticized A's life only from an already assumed ethical perspective. This is of course to beg the question. The same is true of A's quips about the busy man of affairs. Because the views are complete unto themselves, they can only be evaluated from the outside, from the reference point of another view which can never be decisively "proven" to be superior to either. This brings us back to the discussion of the need for *indirect* communication. Because we are dealing here with complete life views whose adoption will alter a person's life at its core, only indirect communication is appropriate. Direct rational argumentation cannot "prove" the case in a logical sense. To say this is already to be "outside" of the Judge's (Hegel's) view.[2]

Let's look then at what can be said of the Judge's views. Tell me, are you a little suspicious? The Judge certainly has things tied up in a neat little bow. And yet there is a ring to his life which is not true. Not, of course, that he is lying to us; he surely believes what he says, or at least he wants to believe it. Perhaps that's it. He sounds like a man more interested in convincing himself than in convincing us. What we need is someone expert at ferreting out self-deception in its most subtle variety, someone even more serious than Judge William. There was once such a person, an abbot of a monastery in the Sinai Desert in the sixth century. His name was John Climacus (John the Climber, John of the Ladder). It was his job as abbot to root out pretense, pride, rationalization, excuse, procrastination, all those so-human responses that lodge themselves between my present self and my goal of "purity of heart." If such a man could be resurrected, what a job he could do on our pompous friend Judge William.[3] In point of fact a man named Johannes Climacus did appear on the scene, and did comment upon our friend the Judge, in a book with the curious title *Concluding Unscientific Postscript.*

> I have read what the Judge has written about marriage in *Either/Or* and in *Stages on Life's Way.* I have read it carefully. It has not surprised me to learn that many who are fully informed about world history and the future of the human race have censured a solution which first makes the matter as difficult as it is before it attempts an explanation. For this I cannot blame the Judge . . . but nevertheless I think that the Judge, supposing I could get hold of him and whisper a little secret in his ear, will concede that there are difficulties he did not take into account. [CUP, p. 161]

What sort of difficulties has the Judge not considered? In its most general he has overlooked (repressed perhaps) the fact that human life as the existing individual lives it is riddled with paradox, with double-bind situations, with ambiguity. This means in practice that on the one hand life will present situations which will passionately demand that one of many actions be chosen and on the other hand there will not be and could never be a clear rule, program, or guideline to follow which will provide the solution. Clarity, order, and harmony can always be achieved in *pure thought,* but as soon as it is a real, existing problem that is being considered, ambiguity is unavoidable. "The paradox is not a concession but a category, an ontological definition which expresses the relation between an existing cognitive spirit and eternal truth" [J&P, p. 3089]. Thus Climacus says, "we shall here posit and expound two theses: (A), a logical system is possible; (B), an existential system is impossible" [CUP, p. 99]. In his adherence to Hegelianism the Judge has tried to implement the idea that the Real (his own life) is the Rational (can be made subject to clear and absolutely certain ethical principles). But is not the Judge's marriage living proof that the clarity and harmony of pure thought can be translated into a life? We should be a little suspicious, I think. The Judge says,

> In general woman has an innate talent . . . for explaining finiteness. When man was created he stood there as master and lord of all nature . . . but he did not comprehend what he was to do with it all. . . . Then was woman created. . . . she knew at once how one had to handle this affair. . . . this was the first comfort bestowed upon man. She drew near to him, humble as a child, joyful as a child,

pensive as a child.... And, lo, her humble comfort
became life's richest joy, her innocent pastimes life's
most beautiful adornment, her childish play life's
deepest meaning. . . . Woman explains finiteness,
man is in chase of infinitude. . . . For this reason I
hate all talk about the emancipation of woman.
[E/O, II, pp. 315–16]

What the Judge has in mind here is that one can always distinguish the active and the passive, the spirited and the
natural, the infinite and the finite. These distinctions mean
different things but are analogous. And these distinctions correspond in the Judge's mind to the male (active, spirited) and
the female (passive, purely natural). It is on this basis that the
Judge's view of marriage rests.

Note, though, that this view corresponds in all but the
language with that of Johannes the Seducer, except that
Johannes has the honesty to be clear about it.[4] He says,

This being of woman . . . is rightly described as
charm, an expression which suggests plant life; she
is a flower, as the poets like to say, and even the
spiritual in her is present in a vegetative manner.
She is wholly subject to Nature and hence only aes-
thetically free. . . . the concept of woman requires
that she be vanquished; the concept of man, that he
be the victor. . . .
My practice has always been impregnated with the
theory that woman is essentially a being for another.
[E/O, I, p. 426]

The Judge says,

I have a home, and this home is not everything, but
I know that I have been everything to my wife. I
know it partly because in all humility she has believed it, partly because I know within myself that I
have been and shall be, so far as one can be everything to another. [E/O, II, p. 82]

The Judge tells us that the highest goal of human life is to
live in the "eternal," that is, to accept and develop one's ethical duty, one's absolute *telos*. Yet the Judge does not blink a
moral eye at the idea that *he* is the "absolute *telos*" of his
wife's life. Theoretically the Judge's marriage has accomplished a "mediated harmony" of two independent individuals, opposed in the sense that each has his or her own

interests. Theoretically it is the Hegelian dialectic in action. In reality, in the ambiguous and paradoxical world of existence, the harmony about which the Judge expounds was purchased at the price of the *suppression* of one of the elements of the dialectical pair. A "mediated harmony" between two existing *individuals* had not been achieved. When two people enter a relationship as independent, qualitatively distinct existing individuals, that relationship remains always like "coiled springs . . . which are what they are only because of qualitatively distinguishing passion" [TA, p. 78].

There are other problems with the Judge's views. It is life's foremost aim, he says, to be a moral person, to be "in the right," and yet life presents us with situations where to wish to be in the right conflicts with the love of others. The Judge loves his wife. Suppose a disagreement arises between them, an offense has been committed. It is indicative of his love for her for him to want to be in the right, to wish that it was she who was in the wrong? Would not the lover say, "It was all my fault, please forgive me"? This case was pointed out to the Judge by an old friend who now held a parish in the bleak hinterlands of Jutland. Perhaps the priest had read John of the Ladder; he surely knows the Judge. How can you be so certain, he asks, that you are "in the right"? Are not you covering up a mass of moral self-doubt? He anticipated the Judge's answer.

> Was this your consolation that you said: One does what one can? Was this not precisely the reason for your disquietude, that you did not know within yourself how much it is a man can do? . . . no earnest doubt, no really deep concern, is put to rest by the saying that one does what one can. [E/O, II, p. 348]

Only the man himself can decide if he is to a certain degree in the right, to a certain degree in the wrong. Yet when he decides this, won't he also be "to a certain degree in the right," etc.? "Or is he when he judges his action a different man from the man who acted?" [E/O, II, p. 349]. To be in the right is to have done one's duty; it is to have done *enough*. In the face of the question "Has one done enough?" it is glib to say that one does what one can. That merely pushes the question back a step. In fact one can never know if one is *in the right*. One cannot then *take pleasure* at doing one's duty—except with the aid of self-deception.

Think of the point the Jutland Priest has made. You live a good, middle-class existence; honest in business; faithful to friends, family and community; generous with those who are in need of your assistance. Is this enough? Mother Theresa *lived* among the poor; others less known have given up everything to work for their fellow man. What precisely exempts you? the Priest asks. "Be reasonable," you say, "I have a life of my own. I do what I can." But how can you be so sure that you have done what you can, when others have done so much more? Isn't it true that your moral complacency is achieved only by avoiding the example of those who have done so much more, while concentrating upon those who have done so much less? To be a moral person can function as the *telos* of one's life only with the support of self-deception.

The Judge also claims to be a Christian, and assumes that there is a perfect consistency between his life as a man of duty and his life as a Christian. Yet the point above about wanting to be in the wrong before one's love applies even more so to God. More important, there are times when ethical duty and religious faith collide. The case of Abraham and Issac provides an example. God commanded Abraham to kill his son, Isaac. Abraham agreed and was fully prepared to carry out the command even though (1) he had no way of being certain on *objective grounds of evidence* that it was God's command, and (2) it was his moral obligation according to any rational system of ethics to protect and preserve the life of his son. It was a temptation of the worst kind.

> What ordinarily tempts a man is that which would keep him from doing his duty, but in this case the temptation is itself the ethical—which would keep him from doing God's will. [FT, p. 70]

The romantics proposed to let individual conscience be the guide to one's moral life. Hegel had demanded that reason be the guide. But in this case, the religious situation, only faith was the guide. There was in Kierkegaard's famous phrase "a teleological suspension of the ethical," that is, an ignoring of the rational moral claims for a higher purpose. In *Fear and Trembling* the religious is put over against the rational ethical with the former taking precedence; and the individual alone in his religious faith is put over against the universal with the former taking precedence. Finally since faith is a matter of will and rational ethics a matter of reason, then will is put over against reason with the former taking precedence. Judge William (Hegel) is the object of each of these points.

Finally Judge William claimed that his belief in the ultimate power of human reason was consistent with his Christianity. But history had shown clearly enough that rationalism and Christianity could get along together only by emasculating the latter. This seemed to have become indisputable with the publication in 1835 of David Strauss' *Life of Jesus.* There was hardly a more controversial book published in the entire nineteenth century (Darwin's *Origin of Species,* 1859, being one obvious exception). What Strauss' colleague C. A. Eschenmayer thought of his work is obvious in the title of the latter's book *The Iscariotism of our Time.*[5] In the early 1840s the University of Copenhagen joined the controversy by offering a prize for an essay that would investigate "the question, if and how far the Christian religion is conditional upon the authority of the books of the New Testament and upon their historical reliability."[6] It was on this point that Strauss' work had been so devastating. He investigated the historical evidence that would support the stories told in the Gospels, and he found it wanting. The only plausible, rational, scientific approach to the Gospel records was, he concluded, to consider them as myths. But this is not to deny the truth of Christianity, he argued, only to point out that it needs reformulating in a language that modern man can assent to. The basic idea remains intact. This was, precisely as Hegel had said, that the human *is* the divine. To think of only the individual person Jesus as divine is to miss the crucial point. Christianity demands, then, not worship by the individual of Jesus, but participation of the individual in the divine, that is, *in humanity.* A rational perspective succeeds therefore in residing with Christianity only by transposing the latter into pure secularism. The worship of the divine becomes service to mankind. The gap between the secular and the transcendent has been closed, by allowing only the secular to remain. Once again there had been no "mediated synthesis" between Christianity—with its central doctrine of the divinity of Jesus—and reason. Christianity and reason collided. What came out of the collision was not a synthesis, but reason intact and Christianity shattered.

To pretend otherwise would be to deceive oneself and others. This is not at this point a criticism of the Hegel-Strauss-Judge William treatment of the problem, but only a criticism of their shared claim to have retained both reason *and* Christianity.

This then seems to be the truth about Judge William's life. For all its talk of God, and of the eternal—religion is, after all, essential to bourgeois life—it is a purely secular doctrine excluding any concept of the transcendent religious. It is secular humanism plain and simple. The Judge says,

> For man's eternal dignity consists in the fact that he can have a history, the divine element in him consists in the fact that he himself, if he will, can impart to this history continuity . . . in such a way that even what has befallen me is by me transformed and translated from necessity to freedom. [E/O, II, p. 254]

This same point can be seen by the content of the Judge's argument against the life of A. His entire point was that A should relinquish his ideals because they were impractical, impossible, would lead ultimately to melancholy and even madness. This included even the Seducer. But the perceptive Climacus points out concerning the Aesthete (the Seducer in particular),

> [whoever] needs the reassurance of a warning lecture in order to see that a standpoint is erroneous, or needs an unfortunate consequence, like madness, suicide, poverty and the like, does not really see anything. Whoever needs that [the Seducer] should become mad or shoot himself in order to see that his standpoint is perdition, does not see it. . . . [CUP, pp. 263–64]

There would be something perverse in trying to convince a sadistic, clever, and successful murderer to forsake this life on the grounds that he would be a good deal happier as an Episcopalian. Yet this is the essence of the Judge's argument. Seeing it in this way may incline one to agree with the wise Frater Taciturnus who says in *Stages on Life's Way,*

> . . . the poetic is glorious, the religious is still more glorious, but whatever falls between them is prattle. . . .[7]

The Judge had collapsed the distinctions between the religious and the ethical, the ethical and the psychological, and in both instances in favor of the latter terms. He resolved the "coiled springs" of the relationship of the individual to the group and woman to man by exhorting the former in each case to submit to the latter. His "mediations" were frauds, and always in favor of the orthodox. In Judge William, "The esthetic ideal is replaced by national taste, yes, town-and-class taste, and the most correct copy of it" [J&P, p. 854]. Marx was not the only mid-nineteenth-century thinker to perceive that grand theories when "seen through" can often turn out to be the productions of a class in service of the tastes of that class.

EIGHT

TWO DIMENSIONAL
LIFE PATTERNS

Y ou have now seen through the Judge, especially the
way that he takes a word with a clear and definite
meaning—for example freedom, individuality, the eternal, the
religious, the ethical, guilt, or sin—and empties out its significance. The result is a system which becomes a gigantic abstract justification for bourgeois taste. And you know that
bourgeois life—whatever its virtues—can never be identified
with the ideal human life. Every bourgeois who even trips
over a moment of reflection screams to himself the words of
the old Peggy Lee song, "Is that all there is?" You have
heard that scream in yourself. Yet you also know that a
self-indulgent, romantic life of intense feelings and kinky experiences would gradually blow your mind apart. What
should you do? "Go into therapy?" And what would the
therapy do? Help you to be satisfied with all the accou-
terments of bourgeois life? Or maybe help you to throw it
all off? But in favor of what? The therapist would help you
"express your feelings," but isn't that one of the problems?
That you have feelings—of disgust, emptiness, nausea, moral
failure, guilt—which if they were expressed would destroy
you and those you love. And after you expressed these
feelings, would they go away? If so, then you could go back
to bourgeois life without the slightest sense of ironic distance.
You would be "back into things." But then all would be lost.
You would have purchased rest at too great a price. Your

problems are not *psychological*. You have no hand-washing obsessions, no delusions, no unrealistic fear of heights, water, or reptiles. Your problem is that first, you are making upon your life a set of vague demands which are not being met, and that second, you don't know concretely what *would* meet the demands. Are you perhaps expecting too much from life? Many people would no doubt give their left arm to have what you have. You feel ashamed sometimes that "with all I have, I'm still not satisfied." But you know better than that. Precisely that thought, "I should be thankful for what I've got," has been used to paper over your doubts once too often. You know now that you've run out of tricks. Career, sex, money, success, talent, beauty, power, health, community service, the children, building a marriage, the boat, the grandchildren, retirement, self-awareness, martinis, books, television, adult education, the degree—they have all failed to provide a focus, a goal, a *telos* for your life. And you know now why, and you are willing despite your modern, liberal attitudes to think about it, what must be done. These things are all *secular*. They are worldly, transient, finite, temporal, homogeneous with each other. They are one-dimensional, *but you are not*. You are a synthesis of all these things *and the Eternal*. The Eternal, the Good, the Transcendent, the Absolute Telos has claim to you; not to just a part of you but to your absolute concern. These other things must find their place in your life only as *relative* goods, goods whose importance depends upon the Eternal's being the absolute *telos* of your life.

But this is ridiculous. It is religion. Religion is for children and old ladies; a crutch for weaklings to get themselves through life; a regression to an infantile dependence upon father; a universal cultural neurosis; an organ of the state to maintain cultural values. Most of all it's just silly; all those archaic rituals; candles burning; all that mumbo-jumbo. If it weren't for the music you'd never set foot inside.

All of a sudden you're strong again. The very thought of religion, and of all the losers who wrap themselves in it, has picked you up. "Was that what I was headed for?" you ask. You're confident again—for a while. Ready to take your turn at the tennis club—one more time. The saving value of the cliché—where on earth would we be without it?

But you remember your promise—no more tricks—and

so you admit that this reaction of yours is the *purest preju-dice*, emanating as a critically undisturbed flow from that liberal, modern mind-set which on other occasions you have scorned. You admit that you are "double-minded," and that you can't have it both ways. You can't admit the hollowness of your sophisticated modernity, and then use it to chase away the specter. "But I just don't know what all those words mean," you protest, and this time honestly. So this then is the question for now, and you're ready to think about it. What does it mean to be a religious person? What are the guarantees? What is the proof? What are the re-wards? the sacrifices? What's in it for me?

First, to the question of what it *means* to be a religious person *in the abstract*. The formula is: a religious person is one who has developed an absolute relationship to the abso-lute *telos*. The word *telos* means "goal," "intended end." An-other expression for this is that the religious person has made his eternal blessedness the absolute *telos* of his life.

This demands some preliminary remarks. It assumes first that existence contains a gigantic chasm which cannot be "mediated"; that is, the chasm between the transcendent (in-finite, eternal) and the secular (finite, temporal). Second, that this chasm is reflected also in the nature of the person, in you. Third, that human life is a battleground in which the person fights with himself concerning which of these he will try to make the absolute *telos* of his life. Fourth, that the at-tempt to make the relative *teloi* of the secular into an abso-lute *telos* of one's life will end in failure (despair). Step number one, then, is to recognize all of this. Thus the reli-gious person is the one who achieves "the simultaneous maintenance of an absolute relationship to the absolute '*Te-los*' and a relative relationship to the relative ends" [CUP, p. 347].[1]

But what is this "eternal blessedness" which should be-come the absolute *telos* of one's life? To try to picture it "in all the magic colors of the imagination" means that one is "a runaway poet, a deserter from the sphere of the aesthetic" [CUP, p. 349]. Eternal blessedness is not a good among oth-ers. To treat it as such is to indicate that it is not an absolute *telos.*

"But," says perhaps a wishful gentleman, an earnest man, who would gladly do something for his eternal

> happiness, "could you not inform me what an eter-
> nal happiness is, briefly, clearly and definitely. Could
> you not describe it 'while I shave' . . ." [CUP, p.
> 351]

Think of an analogy. Suppose someone had been brought up
from infancy in oppression, personal degradation, continuous
betrayal, and human emptiness. During all this, survival skills
have reached a fine honing, and secular success has not
eluded these skills. Now someone says to this hardened survivor, "You must learn to love, to open yourself up, to give
yourself in a relationship." The survivor answers, "Prove to
me that there is such a thing. Describe it precisely. How
does it feel? I want to know what I'm going to get out of it,
before I decide to fall in love. What will my lover offer me
that I can't buy? I can hire someone to hold my hand, cook
my meals, produce children with me, live in my house." You
can only say that the survivor will know it when love happens, and will know also how foolish are these questions.
Note also that the survivor as described will never "fall in
love." It would have to be a "letting go," a risking of himself, a decision. Finally, suppose one day he declares, "Last
night I fell in love," and is smiling. When will the survivor
see his lover again? "I've made an appointment for the third
Wednesday of next month—for the theater." But then it is
not love, for to be in love is to have one's life transformed.

> I do not know whether to laugh or to weep over the
> customary rigmarole: a good living, a pretty wife,
> health, a social position on a level with an alder-
> man—and then, too, an eternal happiness. . . .
> [CUP, p. 350]

And so "If the idea of an eternal happiness does not transform his existence absolutely, he does not stand related to it"
[CUP, p. 352]. This means that to become a religious person
cannot be like becoming a Rotarian; it must rather be to
transform one's entire life. So we don't speak of a religious
"believer" as we would ask concerning UFOs whether someone is a "believer." We speak rather of a religious exister.
"Do you *exist* religiously?" is the question. This means in the
abstract realm of formulae, "Is your eternal blessedness
the absolute *telos* of your life?" where the idea of eternal
blessedness admits of no concrete description in language.

All that can be said at this point is: (1) it is unlike any of the relative goals and (2) it will be recognizable when it is accepted and (3) it demands a complete life change, since the problem "does not consist in testifying about an eternal happiness, but in transforming one's existence into a testimony concerning it" [CUP, p. 353].

What then must one *do* who has become a religious exister? First the exister must practice *resignation.* He must admit his own complete dependence upon, and nothingness in the face of, the Eternal. He must learn to see himself as a "creature." To be a creature is to have been created by another and to be sustained and in debt to that other. It is

> . . . the annihilation by which the individual puts himself out of the way in order to find God, since precisely the individual himself is the hindrance. [CUP, p. 497]

To be religious is to lose one's "species chauvinism." Does "putting aside the things of the world" lead inevitably to the ascetic life as the ideally religious life? The answer is no. The medieval ascetic monk is praiseworthy in that he took seriously the problem of the relationship of relative to absolute ends. But his solution is "both too much and too little; it is too much because it involves a certain presumptuousness over against other men, and it is too little because it is after all a wordly expression" [CUP, p. 440]. The monk tries to *deny* his humanity, his secularity, when the point is to put it in its place, simultaneously maintaining relative relationship to the world and an absolute relationship to the Eternal. This situation has no *essential* outward expression. There is no behavior which "proves" that a person is religious. It is rather a matter of completely transforming one's life inwardly.

This matter of resignation will never be easy; it must involve suffering. Man is tied to the secular as truly as he is called by the Eternal. To wrench himself inwardly from the world is to suffer. It is a humiliation of his pride, constant temptation and tension, and always in the face of the objective uncertainty that it is pure foolishness. To live thus is to live *in the truth,* that is to live *truly.* It is a life of "objective uncertainty held fast in an appropriation-process of the most passionate inwardness" [CUP, p. 182]. It is the life of faith, and such a person is the Knight of Faith. Abraham was such a person, willing to sacrifice the secular focus of his life on the objectively uncertain command of the Eternal. From the aesthetic point of view Abraham was mad; from the ethical view he was evil. Religiously, he was a hero. There is no reconciling these views. The Knight of Faith "looks like a tax collector," yet,

> Let the world give him everything, it is possible that he will see fit to accept it. But he says: "Oh, well," and this "Oh, well" means the absolute respect for the absolute *telos*. If the world takes everything from him, he suffers no doubt; but he says again: "Oh, well"—and this "Oh, well" means the absolute respect for the absolute *telos*. Men do not exist in this fashion when they live immediately in the finite. [CUP, p. 368]

In addition to an inward resignation from the world and the consequent suffering, the decisive mark of the religious person is a sense of total guilt. The word for guilt which Kierkegaard uses [*skyld*] means "debt." The "decisive expression" of the religious exister is the consciousness of one's total debt to the eternal—that one owes oneself, is rightly owned by, the Eternal.[2] It is not then a question of having done this or that for which one is guilty but rather "a question of one's essential relation to existence" [CUP, p. 471].

So there it is, one is religious in proportion to the degree of one's inward resignation, suffering, and consciousness of total indebtedness to the eternal. This will be, more or less, the life of an absolute relation to the eternal and relative relations to finite ends. *Any other life is self-deception.* To live in self-deception is to be double-minded, to be turned in against oneself, to have more than one will. Purity of heart is to will one thing. The argument of Climacus, and of Kierkegaard in *Purity of Heart*, is that only a religious exister, one who wills the Eternal—makes the Eternal his absolute *telos*—can escape double-mindedness. Man cannot live in the secular only and escape from self-deception or despair.

> . . . each one in despairing has two wills, one that he fruitlessly tries wholly to follow and one that he fruitlessly tries wholly to avoid. In this fashion has God . . . insured himself against every rebel-

lion. . . . each rebel against God, in the last instance, is himself reduced to despair. [PH, p. 61]

This is plainly and simply a fact of life for Kierkegaard. It is a fact which in an intellectual sense can be grasped and justified by the kinds of analyses of the human condition which he has provided. But it is also a fact around which a person can build a life. But this would never happen on the basis of intellectual argumentation alone; it demands rather that one appropriate this fact in an act of faith, making it part of one's self. In this case it has become a truth *for one's self;* for as the Priest from Jutland says, "only the truth which edifies is truth for you" [E/O, II, p. 356].

Perhaps the question still nags at your brain, "But what will I get out of it? Will it bring me peace? happiness? rest? What are the rewards?" Kierkegaard answers,

> If a man loves a girl for the sake of her money, who will call him a lover? . . . The Good is one thing; the reward is another. . . . When he, then, wills the Good for the sake of the reward, he does not will one thing but two. [PH, pp. 69–70]

And this is double-mindedness. It is a contradiction within oneself to try to make the Eternal the focus of one's life *in order to* achieve some secular reward. This could only be accomplished through self-deception. In the secular sense the *expectation* of eternal blessedness is the highest reward. "When the individual is no longer content with this, it means that he relapses into wordly wisdom" [CUP, p. 360]. What proof is there that this expectation will be realized, that there even is such a thing as the Eternal? To prove that someone ought to exist religiously is to prove that something ought to be *done*, not merely believed. To prove that an action ought to be done is always to balance off the benefits where each is weighted by its respective likelihood. From a secular perspective, to exist religiously risks everything with no guarantee of benefit. From a purely secular perspective it is irrational. From a religious perspective it is salvation. Which perspective to adopt when addressing the question is the choice which each individual must make, and be accountable for.

Perhaps the severity of this choice can be diminished by *easing into* the religious. Perhaps you think you can try on the religious in dribs and drabs, and see if anything comes of it; experiment in your life with existing religiously as when you enter the cold ocean by dipping in first your little toe, then your big toe. This, of course you have guessed, will not do. "The person who only wills the Good up to a certain degree is double-minded" [PH, p. 104]. Probabilities and degrees belong to the "time order," eternity is an "either/or."

You may at least object that the emphasis upon inwardness, upon changing the inward focus of one's life, leaves one free to *behave* as he would like. It was said in discussing the ascetic that willing the Eternal has no *essential* external expression. But the emphasis there is on the term "essential." There is no external behavior which would prove, certify, ensure—even if done sincerely—that one is willing the Good. However, to will the Good does have implications for your external life. It implies at the very least that you live as an "individual."

To live as an "individual before the Eternal," here are some things to consider. You must earnestly consider your life and consider your life in earnest. That is, you must be serious in the way you think of your own life, and serious in the way you live. Existing religiously, with the consciousness of the Eternal, makes self-deception impossible. To exist religiously is then to be reflective and transparent to oneself. This means among other things to put aside "busyness," that kind of action whose purpose it is to fill up time. The person who has lived in earnest has "lived so that he has hours and times in which he collects his mind, so that his life can win transparency" [PH, p. 183]. "Busyness" is not, of course, an accidental impediment to transparency, but rather a tactic to avoid it. It is a temptation.

To live as an "individual before the Eternal" is to subordinate all human relations to your relation to the Eternal.

> If you are bound to another human being by the holy bond of matrimony do you consider in this intimate relation that still more intimate relation in which you as an individual are related to yourself before God? [PH, p. 187]

> If your marriage is so blessed that you see a family growing up around you, may you be conscious that while you have an intimate relation to your children

you have a still more intimate relation to yourself as
an individual. [PH, p. 188]

As with your spouse and children, so with the world in
general.

> ... do you remember each time you throw yourself
> in this way into the world around you, that in this
> relation, you relate yourself to yourself as an indi-
> vidual with eternal responsibility? Or do you press
> yourself into the crowd, where the one excuses him-
> self with the others.... [PH, p. 190]

The point then is to deal with the world as an individual
person, divorced inwardly from the crowd, always conscious
of one's prime responsibility to the Eternal. "You should not
withdraw and sit brooding over your eternal accounting"
[PH, p. 197], but rather inwardly transform secular en-
deavors from the most trivial to the most intimate by means
of a consciousness of one's being an "individual before the
Eternal."

This will necessarily have an effect upon what you do.
One could not live with a consciousness of the Eternal and
also work at an occupation which was not also a calling.
Consciousness of the Eternal would demand that the produc-
tive labor of one's life be more than merely a money-making
activity. This would not be to live in earnest. Nor would
such an individual be unconcerned about the tactics one uses
to achieve the goals of his labor? In fact, from the standpoint of the Eternal it doesn't matter if a man's secular goals
are achieved, but the means he employs *are* of interest. Man
is not "eternally responsible" for his successes or failures.
"But without exception, he is eternally responsible for the
kind of means he uses" [PH, p. 202]. This rules out even
that little flattery, that small concealment, that little untruth,
the false union, the undeserved admiration, the clever
scheming.

To be an individual before the Eternal is to avoid
wanting to apply to others the rules which you do not apply
to yourself or your group. This means also to avoid judging
others on the basis of worldly associations; that is, to avoid
clannishness, "the enemy of universal humanity." True human unity is based upon the idea that each person stands
alone before the Eternal.

> . . . to will one thing only, genuinely to will the
> Good, as an individual, to will to hold fast to God,
> which things each person without exception is capa-
> ble of doing, this is what unites. [PH, p. 106]

This approach to the questions of ethics, of what should
be done, will not satisfy the legalist. He is the one who
wants rules, both general and precise, to cover any conceivable situation. Without this he will claim not to know what is
to be done. But this demand is itself an evasion, for what he
really wants is to be able to say of any of his actions, "I was
required to do it; it wasn't my fault." The fundamental
question of morality is one of *character*, and character is inwardness. To exist as an individual, conscious of the Eternal,
is to have developed character. The point is not that it does
not matter what such an individual does, but rather that because he has character he can be relied on to do what is
proper. This would not be true of one who had even the
most precise knowledge of the rules and regulations of moral
behavior—were such possible. Raising children to be morally
responsible adults is an example of the problem of ethics.
The point is not to give them a "knowledge" of principles
which will cover every conceivable situation, and have them
follow these principles. Even if that were possible it may not
be desirable. The point is to see to it that the child develops
moral character—basic traits of honesty, seriousness, com-
passion, openness to self, etc. That is the most that can be
hoped for. Moral *behavior* will then take care of itself. The
religiously existing individual has, above all others, character.

Why, you may wonder, has the discussion of religious
consciousness almost systematically avoided the use of the
word "God"? Why resort to such neutral and less specific
terms as "the Eternal," "the absolute *telos*," "the Good,"
etc.? In wondering about this you have probably guessed at
the answer. A discussion of the religious exister must include
such diverse persons as Abraham, Socrates, St. Theresa of
Avila, and Mohammed, as well as those who share their
modes of religious existence. The elements of religious existence described so far capture a core of commonality which
runs throughout these and other religious traditions.[8] It is
unimportant, of course, whether it is the "god" of Socrates,
Abraham, Mohammed, or St. Theresa that one chooses to
relate oneself to. These choices are matters of cultural, psy-

chological, even aesthetic concern. By and large one religion is as good as any other; the point is to *be* as a religious person. Correct? "Liberal claptrap," says Søren Kierkegaard. Such an opinion shows only that one is not related seriously, and therefore absolutely, to the absolute *telos*. One cannot take a position of ironic detachment concerning that to which one is related absolutely. To be a Jew is to reject with one's life (not just one's mind) the efficaciousness of the death of Jesus. To be a Christian is to affirm it with one's life. You cannot then be a Christian, be absolutely related to Jesus as Lord, and still declare, "Of course, Judaism is equally valid." A soldier will *eagerly* sacrifice his life for his country, but not if he believes that the enemy's principles and viewpoints are "equally valid." Once he believes that, his efforts will lack commitment to his country; his seriousness will be directed toward himself and his immediate comrades. If he can't prefer his country to the enemy, at least he can prefer his friends and himself. Patriotism in this case is lost, although he may still fight bravely and well. The "ecumenical" attitude that "one religion's as good as another" is very modern, very liberal, very tolerant, but also very wishy-washy and dishonest. One who affirms it either is not absolutely committed to the absolute *telos*, or does not believe it, or both. To really mean it is to lack religious seriousness.

In fact this is the charge which Kierkegaard levels against the religious existence described above. You may have recoiled from that description because of how seriously it demanded that you take the religious. You wanted the religious to be *part* of your life and to give you rest. Kierkegaard demands that it *be* your life and promises nothing secular in return. You wanted certainty and you didn't even get probabilities. All you got was: You are the kind of being you are; stop running; accept the Eternal in your life; resign inwardly from the finite; endure the suffering which that involves; realize and accept that you are imperfect and owe any perfection to the Eternal. Yet this view, although supremely preferable to those of the romantic and the bourgeois, in fact lacks seriousness. The reasons are the following.

First, this religious consciousness, which Kierkegaard calls "religiousness A," lacks any conception of sin. Kierkegaard delighted in shocking his readers, especially those he suspected of being "modern" and "liberal." There is perhaps nothing so shocking to the liberal temperament than that there may be an ounce of truth contained somewhere in the idea of sin. The very word "sin" conjures up images of pamphlets describing the evils of masturbation and (even "light") petting. Surely modernity (for all its faults) must have taught us one thing rightly; and if there is a core truth running through all modern social thought it is that sin is an idea whose time has passed. But of course if you have followed Kierkegaard this far you know that he is not about to drape the concept of sin with the trappings of repressed sexuality. The concept is too important, and too crucial to human existing, for that type of silliness. Nor will he try to tell you that it is wrong to "commit a sin." To talk about "committing an illness" is foolish, to talk of "committing a sin" is absurd.

To have a (true) conception of sin is to realize that the bond between the human and the Eternal is not an "automatic" one. Man is not *naturally* connected to eternity. Naturally—or as Kierkegaard would say, immediately—man has only a *potential* bond to the Eternal, as well as an actual calling to the Eternal. To be a sinner is to choose to sever one's bond to the Eternal. It is to intentionally turn away from the proper absolute concern of one's life. It is thus to alter radically—meaning at the root, fundamentally—the nature of one's self. Compared to this conception of sin, the concept of guilt in religiousness A is superficial. For guilt was conceived as natural (not a matter of human choice), and nonessential (not related to who I am as an individual).

> Religiousness A makes the thing of existing as strenuous as possible (outside the paradox-religious sphere), but it does not base the relation to an eternal happiness upon one's existence . . . and therefore infinitely more comes out of it than was put into it. [CUP, p. 509]

Second, to have the right concept of sin is to have the clearest possible idea of the absolute difference between man and the Eternal. As long as man was seen as naturally connected to the Eternal irrespective of his individual existence, then he is in a sense a divine being. The idea of sin makes clear the "infinite qualitative difference" between man and the Eternal.

Finally, once this last point is appreciated, it becomes clear that the Eternal is and must be forever out of the reach of the individual acting, willing, deciding on his own. The "yawning qualitative abyss" which separates man from the Eternal is too great a gap for man alone to cross. There can be no immediate relation to the Eternal.

The recognition of these three factors prepares the way for the facts that: only a Christian religious existence fulfills Eternity's calling for the individual self; only the Christian escapes despair; only the Christian is a completed human being; only within a Christian understanding of human living is the predicament of human life clearly understood; only Christianity has a proper conception of sin; only Christianity understands the relation of man to God; only through the life and death of Jesus is it possible to become related to Eternity. Who then is a Christian? Perhaps no one, "Certainly not myself," Kierkegaard would say. Nor indeed is Climacus, although he *understands* all of the above.

To be a Christian is to be contemporaneous with Jesus. This means *at least* that you believe, despite the fact that your reason objects, that Jesus was both God and man. The union of these two infinitely qualitative differences is an Absolute Paradox, the "crucifixion of reason," yet you believe. It means that you recognize Jesus as your Savior, that without the life and death of Jesus you could never reach the Eternal and thus yourself. It means to accept the fact that one is a sinner.

> . . . only consciousness of sin is the way of entrance, is the vision, which, by being absolute respect, can see the gentleness, loving kindness, and compassion of Christianity. [TC, p. 71]

But you may think that because in Christianity God walked the earth it may be possible to *prove* to yourself about Jesus. If only you had lived in the time of Jesus. How easy it was for the early Christians to believe. Not so, says Kierkegaard. It is ludicrous to think that even one who follows Jesus around recording all that happened would then have "proof" that a man is a God. History can teach us nothing about whether Jesus of Nazareth was God.

> Why not? Because one can "know" nothing at all
> about Christ; He is the paradox, the object of faith,
> existing only for faith. But all historical communica-
> tion is communication of "knowledge," hence from
> history one can learn nothing about Christ. [TC, p.
> 28]

This is Kierkegaard's answer to Strauss' *Life of Jesus*. For the Christian, Jesus did exist; Jesus was a person; Jesus was God; this idea is for one's reason an absurdity and thus can- not be understood; it cannot therefore be proven to be true; it can be believed with certainty through the willing act of Christian faith; when it is believed it no longer appears as an absurdity to the person. The object of the Christian's faith is not a doctrine, "for then the relationship would be intellec- tual"; the object of Christian faith is "God's reality in exis- tence as a particular individual, the fact that God has existed as an individual human being" [CUP, p. 290].

But let's look at this idea a different way. One often hears the demand, "Prove there is a God," or "Prove Jesus was God." What is the proper response of the religiously existing person? What first must be decided is the spirit in which the demand is made. Often the challenge comes from one whose interest is in intellectual games, the point being a little mental sparring, a little proof of the sharpness of one's wit. To this the religious person ought to be silent. For sup- pose someone asked you why you married the person you did with a view toward playing with the question of whether it was or was not a foolish move on your part? Your response would be: Some matters are sacred (ulti- mately serious); about these I don't play games; it would be to insult the one I love to intellectually toy in this way with the relationship. There are certain matters about which it is not appropriate to speak except in seriousness. Chessboards and logic problems are for sharpening one's wit, but one's relationship to God is not.

Suppose, though, that the questioner spoke out of a deep-felt need, that the question was thus serious and sin- cere. Here it is appropriate to point out that the questioner is demanding proof in an area in which proof is not only impossible, but out of place. Suppose his question was to prove to him why he should marry the person to whom he has become engaged. Here you would say that the very question indicates that he is not ready to be married to this person. To demand proof that one is in love is to prove that one is not. The relationship to the one you love is not arrived at through the tight deliberations and computations of national thinking. So it is that one's relation to God is not arrived at through the logic of proof or the arguments of the churches' "officials"

> . . . for since God is a personal being, thou canst well conceive how abhorrent it is to Him that people want to wipe his mouth with formulas. . . . precisely because God is personality in the most eminent sense . . . is the official infinitely more loathsome to Him than it is to a woman when she discovers that a man is making love to her out of a book of etiquette. [AC, p. 153]

> . . . any man's development proceeds in this way. Perhaps he does begin with a few reasons, but this is a lower stage. Then he chooses; under the weight of responsibility before God a conviction comes into existence in him through God. Now he is in the positive position. Now he cannot defend or prove his conviction with reasons; it is a self-contradiction, since reasons are lower. No, the matter becomes more fully personal or a matter of personality: his conviction can be defended only ethically, personality—that is by the sacrifices which he is willing to make for it, the fearlessness with which he holds on to it. There is only one proof for the Truth of Christianity—the inward proof, *argumentum spiritus sancti.* [J&P, p. 3608]

Christianity demands then that one transform oneself inwardly, and orient one's life to Jesus as Savior and as *Pattern.* As Savior, Jesus makes eternal blessedness possible. As Pattern, Jesus provides a way of life. "Christ is gift—to this corresponds faith. Besides, He is exemplar—to this corresponds imitation."[4] Kierkegaard provides in *Works of Love* one of the most elegant descriptions of what the imitation of Jesus—the life of Christian love—should be.

The core of a Christian ethic can be stated in the quote from Matthew 22:39, "You shall love your neighbor as yourself." These are nice words for priestly sermons, you think, but not the stuff of which an ethics is made. If we try to think clearly about this, what could it mean? One suggested interpretation has been "the golden rule," which states, "Do unto others as you would have others do unto you." But nothing could be a more dangerous principle of ethics than this. You would perhaps love to have someone give you the opportunity to make a fortune in money by means of a not very great moral indiscretion. Should the principles of ethics require you to make that offer to another, were it in your power? In requiring you to make available if possible to others what you would wish others to make available to you, the golden rule ignores the possibility that what you may desire of others is immoral. Besides, the golden rule says nothing of love, and the Christian requirement is that you shall *love* your neighbor as yourself. It doesn't tell you—directly at least—to *do* anything, it tells you to *love*.

Here, though, is a problem. If love is not an action or a kind of action; if love is an attitude, an emotion, then it makes little sense to command a person to love. Who after all knows more about love than the poet? And in a sense the poet is quite right when he says "that to command love is the greatest foolishness and the most preposterous kind of talk" [WL, p. 63]. For suppose a husband finds that his wife no longer loves him and bellows, "Love me, I *order* you." His foolishness would only be matched by the question "Well, did she obey him?" Love cannot be commanded, because it is not directly under our control. Love is an inclination, a passion; love *happens* to you, as when you "fall in love." This is all true, says Kierkegaard, but it is true of the love of the poets. It is true of erotic, secular love, and of friendship. Secular love has three major characteristics. It is an inclination, it is preferential, and it is selfish.

To say that secular love is preferential means that it isolates one or a few from the many and loves the *preferred one(s)*. People do not have inclinations toward all the others, only some. The preferential nature of love derives from the fact that it is an inclination. Finally secular love, typified in erotic love (romance) and friendship, is selfish. For what does one say about his love when he is "madly in love"? He says,

> That which delights the poet indescribably, namely, that the lover says, "I cannot love anyone else, I cannot give up loving, I cannot give up this love, for it would be the death of me and I would die of love...." [WL, p. 68]

But, you argue, does he not love his beloved as himself?

Certainly he does, but the beloved whom he loves *as himself* is not his neighbor; the beloved is his other-I. Whether we talk of the first-I or the other-I, we do not come a step closer to one's neighbor, for one's neighbor is the first-Thou. [WL, p. 69]

But still a distinction exists between the one who is interested only in himself and the one who loves another.

The distinction which the world makes is namely this: if a person wants to be all by himself in being selfish . . . the world calls it selfishness, but if in selfishness he wants to form a group with several other selfish people, especially with many other selfish people, the world calls it love. . . . What the world honours and loves under the name of love is group selfishness. [WL, p. 123]

There have been those who wished to proclaim a "religion of love." But by this was meant only that the meaning of human life is to be found in human relatedness, whether this meant romantic love, friendship, familial love, "meaningful interpersonal relations," "open relationships," "transpersonal encounters," or what. From the standpoint of Christianity none of this is evil, but neither should it be raised to a status higher than it is. And it *is* all a form of selfishness. Some nonreligious thinkers have shared this opinion, but have taken the tack that selfishness is *the* fundamentally human attitude and can never be transcended. Christianity lets human selfishness stand, as it lets stand the sensual, the erotic. There was a time when Christians "thought that Christianity which as spirit has made a cleft between body and spirit, despised love as sensuality. But this was a misunderstanding, an extravagance of spirituality" [WL, p. 65]. It would be foolish for Christianity to be "scandalized by a drive men have not given themselves" [WL, p. 65]. Christianity lets this stand, but only as what it is. It dethrones the secular and then lets it stand in its proper place.

. . . Christianity has thrust erotic love and friendship from the throne, the love rooted in mood and inclination, preferential love, in order to establish spiritual love in its place, love to one's neighbour. . . . [WL, p. 58]

The key concept in the Christian commandment is that of "neighbor." Who is your neighbor? The answer is simple: your neighbor is every person with whom you have contact. *Humanity* is not your neighbor. To love humanity is a sham, as is every love of an abstraction. Similarly for *mankind, the nation,* etc. Love can only be directed toward an individual. But which individual? Christian love makes no distinctions, allows for no preferences. The Christian commandment requires that each person receive equally your love. It is for this reason that "he who in truth loves his neighbour loves also his enemy" [WL, p. 79]. This simply follows from the fact that one must regard each person equally from the standpoint of Christian love: "No, love does not seek its own, for to seek one's own is simply self-love" [WL, p. 247].

We can, I think, agree with Kierkegaard that the normal kinds of secular love—romance, friendship, familial love—are based upon preference and inclination. They are motivated by strong desires for self-fulfillment, even in those instances in which they are self-sacrificial. In passionate love of any of these kinds the "I-can't-live-without" is very real, indicating that the love fulfills in the lover a deep emotional need. The motivation for the love, its driving force, lies in that need. The love of which the commandment speaks cannot be like this; "you must not love in such a manner that the loss of the beloved would make manifest that you were in despair—that is, you absolutely must not love despairingly" [WL, p. 54]. If your love is not motivated by erotic passion, a feeling for one's own, familial ties, loneliness, etc., what is the motivation to be? Why would one love one's neighbor? The answer is again simple, it is the "royal law." The motive for loving your neighbor is your desire to do what is required of you by the Eternal. Only in this instance, because your love is not dependent upon the vicissitudes of inclination, are you *free* and is your love *secure.* In fact, once this is clear, that your love shall be motivated by your sense of being a creature of the Eternal, the lawgiver, does the concept of "neighbor" become clear. Your neighbor is not one who lives *near* in a geographic sense, or a family sense, or in the sense of "near to my heart." Your neighbor is the person whom you are commanded to love, and this is every person you meet.

If the love of one's neighbor is not motivated by the kinds of feelings that are normally associated with love, what shall be the attitudinal content of this love? What should you as a Christian lover *feel* for the individual who is your neighbor? You need not feel "attracted" to a person, nor need you admire, like, or feel happy when you are with him. But you must see him, experience him, as an *individual* and as a *child of God*. The Christian lover "loves each human being according to the other's individuality" [WL, p. 252]. And the Christian lover approaches his neighbor through the medium of God, as a child of God. This element of the Eternal in every relationship engenders a seriousness which is lacking in secular relationships. Thus a Christian love is always a triadic relation.

> Worldly wisdom thinks that love is a relationship between man and man. Christianity teaches that love is a relationship between: man-God-man, that is, that God is the middle term. [WL, p. 112]

This does not mean that those whom you love with passionate preference as lover, spouse, child, or friend must be neglected. Nor does it mean that the passion need be in any manner diminished. But it does mean that the loved one's status as neighbor, as individual child of God, must take precedence over his status as lover, spouse, child, friend, etc. If the choice ever presented itself between either betraying the other as lover or as neighbor, the worldly passion must give way. To be a Christian means to be *serious* about the Eternal. That means at least that one's Eternal life and that of one's neighbor must always take precedence over the secular. "But divinely understood to love oneself is to love God and truly to love another man is to help him to love God or in loving God" [WL, p. 133].

The last question must be framed carefully. What does the Christian commandment require that I *do* for my neighbor? What are the required actions? To what shall I devote my secular life? Actions, as they say, speak louder than words. An ethic without action is empty. These questions stem from the fact that some of my neighbors live lives of great deprivation and suffering. Ordinary love for a person is expressed in a desire to help that person when in need. What does Christianity require that I *do* for those in need?

Kierkegaard was very careful about how he answered these questions. He lived in a time of "causes." It was a time when politics was taking on the trappings of the sacred, and the religious institutions were increasingly turning toward social problems. A "false mediation" of the Eternal and the temporal was threatened, in favor of the temporal. Salvation has been declared a political problem. All of this ignored the Eternal which was the requirement of the individual, to be *inwardly* oriented toward the Eternal. Kierkegaard saw in well-meaning causes and social programs a threat to the individual, which was as great as any form of depravity. He feared leaving the impression that to be a Christian meant only that one do some good works. So that while it is true that an ethic without action is empty, so it is also true that good works without God-consciousness are Eternally irrelevant. Christianity means *character transformation*; to emphasize good works ran the risk of missing that point. So Kierkegaard, as was his way, said what he believed. If two things needed to be said, he said both. But when it came to deciding which to *emphasize*, he chose on pragmatic grounds. "My task has continually been to provide the existential-corrective" [J&P, p. 708]. He emphasizes always what his readers have forgotten. And what they have forgotten was that "Christianity and worldliness never come to an understanding with one another, even for a moment" [WL, p. 82]. One can never be a Christian and totally "worldly" even if it is a worldly life completely devoted to good works. Kierkegaard wants so intently to stress this that he only very reluctantly even mentions the relation between the Christian and his good works. What is important, he says, is the *attitude* emanating from character. Mercifulness is the Christian *attitude* toward those who suffer.

> Woe unto him who devours the inheritance of widows and orphans, but woe also to the preachers who are silent about mercifulness in order to talk about charity. Preaching should be solely and only about mercifulness. If you know how to speak effectually *about this*, charity will follow of itself and come by itself to the degree to which the individual is capable. [WL, p. 292]
>
> It follows naturally of itself that if a merciful person can do something, he does it most gladly. But we do

not wish to concentrate attention upon this. . . .
[WL, p. 300]

The point is for the individual Christian to orient himself
properly to God. From this, Christian love of his neighbor
will follow, and from the latter will naturally flow charitable
works. The works themselves *prove* nothing, nor do they
earn anything. They are simply the natural expression of a
Christian love for the suffering neighbor. Christianity is not
a *social* movement. The equality of which it speaks is the
Eternal equality of all individuals. It therefore neither op-
poses nor promotes political movements aimed at secular
equality. Even though caste systems such as serfdom were
"abominable," "ungodly," a "horror," etc., still there cannot
be life

> . . . without the distinctions of earthly life which
> belong to each individual, whether by virtue of
> birth, position, circumstance, education, etc.—no one
> of us is pure or essential man. Christianity is too
> earnest to present fables about pure man—it wants
> only to make man pure. . . . [WL, p. 81]

Christianity, then, will not take differences away, neither the
distinction of poverty nor that of social position. But on the
other hand, Christianity will not in partiality side with any
temporal distinction.

The Christian ethic, then, is an ethic of love of God.
Love of God engenders the concept of neighbor and the
commandment to love one's neighbor. Love of neighbor
gives rise to mercifulness, which will naturally result in char-
ity as a matter of course. The Christian commandment is,
then, "Love God above all else, and love thy neighbor as
thyself."

Who then are these Christians? Show me just one. Perhaps no one is a Christian, says Kierkegaard, certainly not
the tradesman who says, "Everyone cheats," and then dresses
for church. Not even Judge William, hero of bourgeois virtue. The thought that "the public" could be so foolish as to
think themselves Christians prompted Kierkegaard to launch
a vicious attack upon the orthodox Lutheranism of his time.
The attack ended only with his death in 1855. When you
combine the ideas (1) that Christianity is a matter of *self*-
transformation and (2) the internal is not the external, then
it follows that no one can decisively point and say, "I have

proof, he is a Christian." Nor would anyone who happened to be a Christian be certain of that fact in the sense of having proved it to himself. Only faith is possible, only an objective uncertainty believed as the result of an act of will.

NINE

BEGINNINGS

When the hideous Medusa was beheaded by Perseus, out from her trunk sprang Pegasus, the winged horse. He was the son of Poseidon and bearer of the thunderbolts of Zeus. By merely striking Mount Helicon with his hoof, Pegasus created the sacred spring of Hippocene, the source of poetic truth and rapture. Kierkegaard wonders,

> Who thinks of hitching Pegasus and an old nag together to one carriage for a ride? And yet this is what it is to exist [*existere*] for one compounded of finitude and infinitude! [J&P, I, 55]

This is an apt metaphor for the situation which every individual must confront. It is a condition of self-division, built into every person's nature as a human being. It is his most fundamental obligation for each person to face this self-conflict, to live with it, to endure the anxiety which it breeds, to resist the temptation to retreat from it into a less-than-human life, that is, to be a genuine individual. The self-conflict between the sublime and the mundane exists at all levels of the individual's life. The task of properly relating them is life's dialectic, to choose to avoid this task is human failure (despair, sin).

It is a tragic mistake, therefore, to think of the ideal human life in terms denoting harmony, peace, contentment, natural integration, bliss, or any such concept. Man is neither flower nor angel. Nor is man a flower with an angel inside, a ghost in a machine. It is not man's psychophysical division

157

that is being referred to. The self is not a static entity, but a task, an obligation. To speak of a self-conflict is to point to the paradoxical nature of this human task. It is a man's power and obligation to single himself out of the group, to be able always to say, "I, and no one else, am me" (individuality); and yet it is his task to simultaneously be one of a group (sociality). It is man's power and obligation to isolate and examine his own values as if they were merely being entertained (irony); and yet it is his task to be passionately earnest about those values (commitment). It is man's power to envision realities, projects, and sentiments which transcend the everyday (infinitude); and yet recognize that in many ways existence is immutable (finitude). It is within a man's power to envision himself in an indefinitely large number of future situations, every one distinct from his present (possibility); but it is his task to distinguish between those futures which are real possibilities and those which are possibilities for the imagination only (necessity). Finally it is man's obligation to simultaneously maintain an absolute commitment to his own absolute *telos* (eternity); while simultaneously maintaining his commitments to relative, secular values (temporality). A man's life is ambiguity and paradox. It is *human* existence, characterized by a giant chasm separating the sublime and the mundane. Astride the chasm is the power of human will, spirit. To attempt to destroy the chasm either by merging the sides or by living on one side only is despair. Is it any wonder then that man is a creature beset by anxiety? Is it a fact to bemoan? What kind of naiveté does it take to believe that in spite of all the contradictory demands, a genuine life of peace and contentment is possible?

One hears it said that Freud was a "pessimistic" thinker; that he espoused a "tragic" view of human life, obviously suffering from remnants of romanticism. This judgment refers minimally to Freud's view that repression is a cultural necessity, and that conflict is therefore inevitable between instinctual needs and the ego. But it refers also to Freud's views on the goals of therapy. At best, says Freud, therapy can remove those forms of neurotic defense which most severely restrict the patient's life, freeing him to experience the normal tensions and pains of human existence. By what criterion is this view to be properly judged pessimistic, morbid, or tragic? It is difficult to escape the conclusion that any view which does not posit the possibility of an integrated blissful humanity, or of a stable human contentment, would be termed "tragic." Freud was too subtle a thinker to espouse such eighteenth-century nonsense.

How much more "morbid" must Kierkegaard's view be, on this way of thinking! Anxiety, says Kierkegaard, does not just *happen* to be a part of human life, it is an essential part. Without it, human life ceases to be human. Even if we could be rid of anxiety, we *should* prefer not to be, for the victory would be pyrrhic. The price would be to remove the "human" from life. This is surely a more fundamental pessimism than Freud's.

Yet there are other points of view on the matter. The possibility of despair is man's curse, says Kierkegaard, but also his eternal dignity. Kierkegaard's view of human nature is dialectical. Every characteristic has its polar opposite. The fact that human life means inevitable anxiety would be senseless without anxiety's dialectical partner, freedom. While emphasizing the seeming paradoxical condition of man's human situation, Kierkegaard reveals himself as a thinker who takes the human individual seriously, and on his own terms. To accept the Kierkegaardian vision is to accept anxiety, but it is also to accept the idea that to be an individual is to be something unique, important, and deserving of ultimate respect. This cannot be said, I believe, either of the reductionist theories that would reduce the individual to some natural system nor of the "humanistic" psychologies of peak experiences. Each of these is nihilistic in both theory and practice. On Kierkegaard's grounds, both constitute insults to the individual. Kierkegaard the thinker takes human life seriously, and within his thought is the idea that it is each person's obligation to take his own life seriously. To think within Kierkegaardian categories is to believe that men are capable of great and fundamental successes in their lives, for which credit is due them; but it is also to believe that men are capable of choosing the most perverse degradations, for which they are deserving of punishment. It is not possible to take human life or the human individual more seriously than this. If Kierkegaard's thought seems to revoke with one hand the possibility of stable contentedness, it returns with the other hand a unique human dignity. As a vision this is not depressing, but rather edifying.

One may be tempted to object here that it is a simple matter for a thinker to treat human anxiety and suffering lightly when his view contains also the promise of salvation.

This is a criticism heard of medieval Christianity, which, so it is said, dismissed the suffering of the poor with the pious incantation that "the first shall be last." But however this may or may not fit the medieval situation, it has nothing to do with Kierkegaard's views. First, Kierkegaard never dismisses human anxiety as unimportant; his claim is only that it is an inevitable concomitant of genuine human life. Second, Kierkegaard never presents salvation or eternal blessedness as a *reason* to choose the eternal. The world of practical reasons, calculations of risk and utility, has no place as an approach to God. If one is tied to the perspective of practical reasoning, there is no rationale for choosing to exist religiously.

Kierkegaard's philosophy provides no formulas for living, and makes no promises. What it does is provide a philosophical theory of value within which a concept of genuine human living is developed. Second, it provides a remarkably varied description of the strategies of deception which are employed in order to escape genuine human living. And third, it provides a host of "insights" into all aspects of human living, from marriage and childrearing to politics.

There is a story of a man who dreamed for years of an extended visit to Paris, to live on the left bank, to absorb Parisian life as it really is. Shortly before the long-awaited departure he canceled his trip, confidently declaring that it was no longer necessary. He had just completed reading the *Michelin Green Guide to Paris*.

Do you think that you now "understand Kierkegaard"? If so this book has failed. It claims only to be a guide, a series of maps, an index of phrases with translations. Its purpose is not to replace the visit but to encourage it, and make it more fruitful. Kierkegaard's authorship is as vast and complex as any European city. To be appreciated it must be confronted. To be beneficial it must be experienced. What follows is the last installment, then, of the guide.

Let us assume now that you are prepared to dedicate some time and effort to the task of confronting Kierkegaard's authorship. Where and how will you begin? Step one is *Either/Or*. This is the cornerstone of Kierkegaard's thought in that it is a description of the two ways of living from which he intends to "convert" his reader. In reading Volume One, keep in mind the image of the German romantic, witty, arrogant, selfish, melancholic, disarming, contradictory, lover of the arts, moody, childish, and "ironic."

Volume One introduces you to this life. The character A is the most sophisticated "aesthete" ever conceived. He is a remarkable person, a man to make any cocktail party a success. A's life is exhibited artistically in Volume One, never described nor directly criticized. In form, Volume One is an "arabesque," as befits its content. This means, though, that you should expect to find no surface order to the presentation. A is a poet, not a systematic philosopher. Volume Two presents what seems to be the only alternative to the life of A. This is the life of social and civic virtue. Judge William is a bourgeois saint. He writes two long letters to A. "On the Aesthetic Validity of Marriage" attempts to show A that bourgeois marriage can provide all the good elements of romantic love, and more. The Judge is a "philosopher," meaning here that he is pedantic, wordy, and systematic. His argument is an application of the Hegelian concept of mediation. The second letter is more general, and more direct in its attack upon A's life. Recall that any attack must be made from some system of values. Judge William's attack upon A is the attack which any well-meaning and intelligent bourgeois would advance. See if you agree. *Either/Or* ends with a letter from a rural priest to Judge William. Kierkegaard provides here a hint of his dissatisfaction with the Judge's life. It also serves to point out that the Judge's "either/or" has not touched all the bases. The priest's letter remains, though, only a hint of things to come.

Upon completion of *Either/Or* you may wish to pursue one or another of the themes contained in it. If the concept of human love interests you, Parts I and II of *Stages on Life's Way* again takes up that theme, and again from a purely secular perspective. The alternatives here are the same as in *Either/Or*. Human love from a religious perspective is dealt with in *Works of Love*. You will note the stylistic differences between the treatments of romantic vs. bourgeois love, and again between each of these and religious love. *Works of Love* is the only one of these books which is not pseudonymous, presenting as it does the religious perspective.

If, however, you wish to develop a better understanding of the framework from which the alternatives presented in *Either/Or* are to be rejected, then you should turn to *Sickness unto Death*. This is the most theoretical of Kierkegaard's treatments of the human self, and of the ways it goes wrong. The language is "philosophical," as befits its topic, but this unfortunately meant, in the nineteenth century, Hegelian. The work, therefore, is very difficult if for no other reason than the terminology. Keep in mind always the dual character of despair, as both a psychic disorder (the psychological) and as a spiritual disorder (the moral and religious). This dual character makes *Sickness unto Death* a different kind of work from the usual twentieth-century social science, which has tried so hard to avoid the moral and spiritual aspects of human living. Having struggled through *Sickness unto Death*—and it will be a struggle—you should be prepared to take on any of the rest of the works, with the exceptions of *Philosophical Fragments* and *Concluding Unscientific Postscript*. You could read *Fear and Trembling*, which is a very dramatic and beautifully written investigation of religious faith within the framework of the story of Abraham and Isaac. If you are still uneasy reading a religious work, that is, a work written from the religious perspective, *Fear and Trembling* is a good place to get over that prejudice. If you are interested in the application of Kierkegaard's vision of individual human life to social concerns, you could now read *Two Ages*. If you would like an inkling of the way in which Kierkegaard himself views the whole of his authorship, he deals with this in *Point of View*. Recall that all of this is, in Kierkegaard's mind, a preparation. Its function is to break down some of the myths, prejudices, and modes of interpretation which you have acquired by being bombarded continually by modern, mass culture, the culture of secularism, profaneness, and superficiality. It is a simple fact, in Kierkegaard's mind, that you cannot live within this perspective and exist religiously. Likewise, unless that perspective is shaken, religiously oriented writings will be senseless to you. You can test yourself on this question with any of the *Edifying Discourses* or the work which is perhaps Kierkegaard's most beautiful, *Works of Love*.

Finally, let me mention secondary sources. The best beginning introduction is Walter Sikes' *On Becoming the Truth*. A step more advanced is Mark Taylor's *Kierkegaard's Pseudonymous Authorship*. Finally, the best work in English, is Gregor Malantschuk's *Kierkegaard's Thought*. There are, of course, many other works about Kierkegaard, some of which have been mentioned in the notes. Secondary sources must be used properly, to clarify specific points, and never as a substitute for the text itself. This is not true of all philosophers, some of whom are better understood through secondary sources for all but the experts. Because of Kierkegaard's purpose, the beauty of his writing, and the excellence of the translations, this is not at all true in his case. It is, indeed, the furthest from the truth.

If then you are so inclined, take this book, use it as a map, and learn about yourself. The choice is yours.

NOTES

Introduction

1. Ernest Becker, *The Denial of Death* (New York: Free Press, 1973), p. 68. Psychologists O. H. Mowrer, Rollo May, and Robert Coles have all speculated that an understanding of Kierkegaard's insights into human living had to wait upon the developments attributed to Freud. See Mowrer, *Learning Theory and Personality Dynamics* (New York: Ronald Press, 1950), May, *The Meaning of Anxiety* (New York: Ronald Press, 1950), and Coles, *Erik H. Erikson: The Growth of His Work* (Boston: Little, Brown, 1970).

Chapter One: To Be a Rebel

1. The life of Søren Kierkegaard (1813–1855) has been very completely presented in Josiah Thompson's *Kierkegaard* (New York: Alfred A. Knopf, 1973), although my preference remains with the old standby, Walter Lowrie's *A Short Life of Kierkegaard* (Princeton: Princeton University Press, 1942).

2. Lord Byron (1788–1824) had died while working in Greece for the forces of unification. His secret related to his incestuous relationship with his half sister. He was born with a club foot.

3. Frederic Ewen, ed., *The Poetry of Heinrich Heine* (New York: Citadel, 1969), p. 31. See also C. P. McGill, "Young Germany: A Revaluation," in J. Boyd et al., *German Studies* (Oxford: Basil Blackwell, 1952).

4. For an account of the group, see A. Sidgwick, *Caroline Schlegel and Her Friends* (London: T. Fisher Unwin, 1897). See also the chapter on "Women's Rights" in G. P. Gooch, *Germany and the French Revolution* (New York: Russell and Russell, 1966); Hans Eichner, *Friedrich Schlegel* (New York: Twayne, 1968).

5. I have discussed the relation of German romanticism to

Kierkegaard in "The German Romantic Background of Kierkegaard's Psychology," *Southern Journal of Philosophy* 5:16 (1978).

6. Friedrich Hölderlin, *Hyperion; or the Hermit in Greece*, trans. W. R. Trask (New York: New American Library, 1965).

7. Ibid., p. 30.

8. There was a great deal of interest in mental illness during this period, accompanied by a somewhat idealized view of insanity as a source of new and genuine insight. As a result the care of the mentally ill began to improve. See F. Alexander and S. Selesnick, *History of Psychiatry* (New York: Harper and Row, 1966), ch. 9.

9. Hölderlin, *Hyperion*, p. 99.

10. Ibid., p. 128.

11. Ibid., p. 131.

12. This was true of *Hyperion*, of *Sorrows of Young Werther*, of Schlegel's *Lucinde*, and to a lesser extent of Kierkegaard's *Either/Or*.

13. Friedrich Schlegel, *Dialogue on Poetry*, trans. E. B. R. Struc (University Park: Pennsylvania State University Press, 1968) p. 159.

14. N. H. Dole, ed., *The Works of Friedrich Schiller* (Boston: Wyman Fogg, 1902). For an excellent account of this period see M. H. Abrams, *Natural Supernaturalism* (New York: Norton, 1971).

15. See Hans Eichner, "Friedrich Schlegel's Theory of Romantic Poetry," *Publications of the Modern Language Association* 71 (1959); Raymond Immerwahr, "The Word 'Romantic' and its History," in S. Prawer, ed., *The Romantic Period in Germany* (New York: Schocken, 1970); and A. O. Lovejoy, "The Meaning of 'Romantic' in Early German Romanticism," in his *Essays in the History of Ideas* (New York: Putnam, 1948).

16. Friedrich Schlegel, *Lyceum Fragments*, in P. Firchow, trans., *Lucinde and the Fragments* (Minneapolis: University of Minnesota Press, 1971), p. 148.

17. Ibid., p. 147.

18. Ibid., p. 149.

19. Ibid., p. 35. Compare Byron's later line from *Don Juan*, XIII, 95 (1824), "Society is now one polished horde formed of two mighty tribes, the bores and the bored," and the line from "A" who is Kierkegaard's romantic character, "All men are bores. The word itself suggests the possibility of a subdivision. . . . Those who do not bore themselves usually bore others, while those who bore themselves entertain others" (E/O, I, 284).

20. Schlegel, *Lyceum Fragments*, p. 46.

21. Ibid., p. 78.

22. Frederick Engels, in fact, had nothing but scorn for the

Young Germany romantics. He gloated that they were soon to be supplanted by the left-wing Hegelians.

23. Schiller wrote to his friend Goethe of *Lucinde,* "It is the acme of modern formlessness and unnaturalness. . . . It is impossible to read it through because its empty gabble makes one ill." Quoted in Sidgwick, *Caroline Schlegel,* p. 161.

Chapter Two: The Discreet Charm of the Bourgeoisie

1. There are different minds about Hegel's politics. The Marxist Herbert Marcuse reads Hegel's thought as genuinely revolutionary. Karl Popper, on the other hand, reads Hegelianism as a defender of the status quo, any status quo. See *Reason and Revolution* (Boston: Beacon, 1941); and *The Open Society and Its Enemies,* vol. 2 (New York: Harper and Row, 1962), respectively. The middle ground is occupied by two excellent expository works: J. N. Findlay, *Hegel: a Re-Examination* (New York: Collier, 1962); and Charles Taylor, *Hegel and Modern Society* (Cambridge: Cambridge University Press, 1979). As we shall see, Kierkegaard understands Hegelianism to be a gigantic apology for bourgeois life, "town and country taste" as he put it.

2. Quoted in Popper, *Open Society,* vol. 2, p. 233.

3. The phrase itself is associated with the theory of "recapitulation" of the German biologist Ernst Haeckel (1834–1919), born three years after Hegel's death. The most important twentieth-century thinker to employ the ontogeny-phylogeny parallel with regard to individual cognitive development and the history of ideas is Jean Piaget (1896–1980). He says, "The fundamental hypothesis of genetic epistemology is that there is a parallelism between the progress made in the logical and rational organization of knowledge and the corresponding formative psychological processes." See his *Genetic Epistemology* (New York: W. Norton, 1970), p. 13. Why no one has remarked upon the relations between Hegel and Piaget is difficult to understand.

4. The nineteenth-century phrase "to have spirit" or "to be spirit" does not mean to be *a* spirit. It has nothing to do with ghosts. It is similar to our phrase "to be spirited," meaning to have a mind of one's own, to be independent, self-controlling, etc. To have spirit is associated therefore with freedom and self-knowledge.

5. We are following the dialectic as presented in Hegel's *The Philosophy of Right,* trans. T. M. Knox (Oxford: Oxford University Press, 1942), and *Encyclopedia of Philosophy* by Hegel, trans. G. E. Mueller (New York: Philosophical Library, 1959).

6. Herbert Marcuse is the chief defender of the view that Hegel's thought is truly radical. Concerning this portion of

Hegel's thought, Marcuse says that Hegel "is guilty not so much of being servile as of betraying his highest philosophical ideas." *Reason and Revolution*, p. 218.

7. Hegel, *Encyclopedia*, p. 236.

8. One is reminded of the innocent flower child of the early 1960s whose do-your-own-thing motto was employed in a different direction by Charles Manson and his "family."

9. Hegel, *Encyclopedia*, p. 248. This is an apt description for the litigiousness of our contemporary scene.

10. Ibid., p. 245–47.

11. G. W. F. Hegel, *The Phenomenology of Mind*, trans. J. B. Baillie (New York: Harper and Row, 1967), p. 758. There is a fine discussion of this in Patrick Masterson, *Atheism and Alienation* (South Bend: University of Notre Dame, 1971). For a more complete treatment, see E. L. Fackenheim, *The Religious Dimension in Hegel's Thought* (Bloomington: Indiana University Press, 1967).

Chapter Three:
To Communicate the Truth

1. Kierkegaard's will dated in 1849 leaves all of his possessions to Regine, to be distributed to the poor should she not want them. See LD, p. 33.

2. It is often claimed that Kierkegaard had a doctrine of three stages: the aesthetic, the ethical, and the religious. There is little agreement, though, on what the stages are stages of. For a discussion of most of the existing interpretations, see Mark Taylor, *Kierkegaard's Pseudonymous Authorship* (Princeton: Princeton University Press, 1975). My own thoughts on the matter appear in "Between the Aesthetic and the Ethical in *Either/Or*," *Philosophy Today* 23 (1979).

Chapter Four:
What Is a Person After All?

1. The exception in the latter case is the question of abortion, which hinges to some extent upon the issue of whether the unborn fetus is a person.

2. The best account of Hobbes' concept of the person, of how it derived from his view of nature, and of its implications is found in J. W. N. Watkins, *Hobbes' System of Ideas* (New York: Barnes & Noble, 1965).

3. This id-ego-superego framework is referred to as Freud's "structural" account of the person and is associated with the third phase in the development and integration of his psychoanalytic theory. The phase began in 1923 with *The Ego and the Id* and

was completed in 1926 with *The Problem of Anxiety*. See Theodore Mischel, "Understanding Neurotic Behavior: From Mechanism to Intentionality," in T. Mischel, ed., *Understanding Other Persons* (Oxford: Basil Blackwell, 1974); and Heinz Hartmann, *Essays on Ego Psychology* (New York: International University Press, 1964).

4. The term "possibility" in the brackets replaces Kierkegaard's term "freedom" which is widely considered to have been a slip of the great man's pen. The other bracketed expressions are in the text.

5. For a development of the idea of existential problems in contrast to pathological problems, see Paul Tillich, *The Courage to Be* (New Haven: Yale University Press, 1952); and J. F. T. Bugental, *The Search for Authenticity* (New York: Holt, Rinehart and Winston, 1965).

6. The term is Tillich's. See *Courage to Be*.

7. Ernest S. Wolf, "Irrationality in a Psychoanalytic Psychology of the Self," in Theodore Mischel, ed., *The Self: Psychological and Philosophical Perspectives* (Totowa, N. J.: Rowman and Littlefield, 1977). The same point is made by Otto Kernberg, *Borderline Conditions and Pathological Narcissism* (New York: Jason Aronson, 1975).

8. The point about Freud is in Rollo May, *Love and Will* (New York: Norton, 1969); a more detailed treatment is found in W. Barrett and D. Yankelovich, *Ego and Instinct: Psychoanalysis and the Science of Man* (New York: Random House, 1971). On the philosophical materials relating to personal causality, see R. Taylor, *Action and Purpose* (Englewood Cliffs, N. J.: Prentice Hall, 1967); see also R. Chisolm, *Person and Object: A Metaphysical Study* (LaSalle, Ill.: Open Court, 1977); and finally R. Harré and P. Secord, *The Explanation of Social Behavior* (Oxford: Blackwell, 1972).

9. The Danish word *angest* is translated in the present edition as "dread." The new edition will employ the term "anxiety" rather than "dread." Although my sympathies remain with "dread" I have used the two interchangeably in the present text.

10. It should also be noted that it was very common in the eighteenth and nineteenth centuries to frame questions about the origins of man and of self in the context of Biblical history. G. E. Lessing (1729–1781), J. G. Herder (1744–1803), I. Kant (1724–1804), F. W. Schelling (1775–1854), and F. Schiller 1759–1805) had all done it. On this point see Abrams, *Natural Supernaturalism*.

11. S. Freud, "Two Principles of Mental Functioning," in S. Freud, *General Psychological Theory* (New York: Collier Books, 1963), p. 22. Kierkegaard is even closer to Freud in the following: "In immediacy, the most false and the most true are equally true; in immediacy, the most possible and the most impossible

are equally actual. As long as this confusion continues without collision, consciousness does not really exist. . . . it is exactly in the collision that consciousness arises. . . ." Quoted from the untranslated papers in Kresten Nordentoft, *Kierkegaard's Psychology*, trans. B. H. Kirmmse (Pittsburgh: Duquesne University Press, 1978), p. 82. In appreciating this statement it should be noted that the term "consciousness" as used by Kierkegaard has a very strong reflexive element. It includes, that is, self-consciousness, so that what is being addressed is the origins of the self-concept.

12. There is oddly very little experimental or observational work on the development of the self, or sense of self, even in the Piagetian tradition. An exception is C. Guardo and J. Bohan, "Development of a Sense of Self-Identity in Children," *Child Development* 42 (1971).

Chapter Five:
A Theory of Human Corruption

1. We are referring here to Freud's later theories of anxiety. For the distinction in question, see Herbert Fingarette's marvelous book *The Self in Transformation* (New York: Harper and Row, 1963), ch. 2.

2. Analogously, Fingarette says of Freud's theory of (structural) anxiety, ". . . anxiety is the other face of ego . . . it *is* ego-disintegration." Ibid., p. 73.

3. Becker, *Denial of Death*, p. 78.

4. See, for example, David Shapiro, *Neurotic Styles* (New York: Basic Books, 1965). Throughout his writings Kierkegaard points out the specific forms of madness that the extreme of any 'life view" or "cognitive style" will assume.

5. The concept of self-deception has not received the attention it deserves among psychologists. An exception is Roy Schafer, who claims that it is the key to understanding all defensive (neurotic) activity. See his *A New Language for Psychoanalysis* (New Haven: Yale University Press, 1976). My own account is influenced by Herbert Fingarette's *Self-Deception* (New York: Humanities Press, 1969).

6. Schafer interprets self-deception as a case of faulty self-observation which is based upon some sort of bias. The word "bias" refers to every variety of defensive distortion. He has succeeded therefore in coming full circle, since he had intended to explain the idea of defensive activity by means of the concept of self-deception. *New Language*, p. 238.

7. The idea that the road of self-discovery will allow no turning back was one of the central ideas of later romanticism—

that life is a spiral journey, accompanied always by both a nostalgia for the past and a necessity of moving forward.

8. This is an apt description of Sartrean existential philosophy with its slogans "existence precedes essence," "Man is condemned to be free," etc. See Jean-Paul Sartre, *Existentialism and Human Emotions* (New York: Philosophical Library, 1957). In practice it is the person for whom life is a series of "trips," "happenings," of things the person is today "into," without continuity or purpose.

9. Perhaps you agree with this last discussion when applied to such large-scale systems of value as those mentioned, but not when applied to that model of objectivity—science. If philosophers can be trusted, though, it applies there also. The first half of this century was spent, in Anglo-American philosophical circles, trying to explicate the purely objective process of scientific proof. The second half has been spent in a devastating critique of that program. That science (yes, even physics) contains elements of human subjectivity is now widely accepted. A good introductory account of this development is found in H. I. Brown, *Perception, Theory and Commitment: The New Philosophy of Science* (Chicago: University of Chicago Press, 1977); a more sophisticated treatment is in F. Suppe, *The Structure of Scientific Theories* (Urbana: University of Illinois Press, 1977). Kierkegaard's point is that human subjectivity, human will, the leap of faith, is involved in all important human activities.

Chapter Six:
The Individual—in One Dimension

1. Ivan Illich notes the manner in which modern man has become almost totally passive with respect to the care of his own body, by turning this care over to the medical profession. To imply, though, that this somehow results from the practice of medicine misses the mark. See his *Medical Nemesis* (New York: Pantheon, 1976).

2. Quoted in Nordentoft, *Kierkegaard's Philosophy*, p. 212.

3. Christopher Lasch, *Haven in a Heartless World* (New York: Basic Books, 1977), p. 137.

4. L. Yablonsky, *The Extra-Sex Factor* (New York: Time Books, 1978); see also A. Pietropinto and J. Simenauer, *Husbands and Wives: A Nationwide Survey* (New York: Time Books, 1978).

5. In the battle of Marengo, June 14, 1800, Napoleon pulled victory from the jaws of defeat in northern Italy after a surprise attack by the Austrians.

6. Paul Tillich dates the symbolic beginning of the movement known as existential philosophy with these lectures by

Schelling. See his "Existential Philosophy," *Journal of the History of Ideas* 5 (1944).

7. Northrop Frye cites *Either/Or* as a prime example of an "anatomy" or "Menippean satire" where the latter as a mode of fiction corresponds strikingly to Schlegel's "arabesque." See Frye's *Anatomy of Criticism* (Princeton: Princeton University Press, 1957), p. 313.

8. The first part of Volume One of *Either/Or* is a set of aphorisms entitled "diapsalmata" or refrains. Schlegel had thought that the aphorism was the most romantic of genres in that it presents a flash of insight in a brief paragraph with no argument, and then moves on to the next topic. As a way of communicating the aphorism is spontaneous, insightful, discontinuous with what comes before or after, and thus is free in the romantic sense of the term.

9. Compare this to Schlegel's "Idyl of Idleness" in *Lucinde*. Kierkegaard's true opinion of this idleness is found in *Concept of Irony*, where he describes it as a "lapsing into an aesthetic stupor which appears as the designation for what it is to live poetically." (CI, p. 311).

10. Wolf, "Irrationality in a Psychoanalytic Psychology of the Self."

11. Kernberg, *Borderline Conditions*, p. 264.

12. Thomas Szaz, *The Second Sin* (New York: Anchor, 1973), p. 42.

13. Once again we are back to the point that unless the person is conceived to be in control of his own life, no sense can be made of that life.

14. For a discussion of some of the philosophical issues surrounding the practice of punishment, see H. L. A. Hart, *Punishment and Responsibility* (Oxford: Clarendon Press, 1968).

15. Theodore Roszak makes the same point for opposite purposes. He finds the "redeeming moral quality" of the self-indulgence of the 1970s to be precisely that there is no "sense of sin." See his *Person/Planet* (New York: Anchor, 1977), ch. 3.

16. Quoted in Lasch, *Haven*, p. 215. Describing the techniques of the "human potential movement," Donald Stone writes that they "are designed to focus attention on an immediate situation in order to stay in the present time in the present continuum of awareness. This is frequently called . . . 'present centeredness' or 'going with the flow.'" In "The Human Potential Movement," in R. Bellah and C. Glock, eds., *The New Religious Consciousness* (Berkeley: University of California Press, 1976), p. 103. Note how the two catch phrases indicate the connection between living in the present and living passively.

17. Lasch, *Haven*, p. 139.

18. There is an interesting analysis of life as the search for

the "perfect moment" in Jean-Paul Sartre *Nausea* (New York: New Directions, 1964).

19. Quoted in Stone, "Human Potential Movement," p. 97.

Chapter Seven:
The Group—In One Dimension

1. The Judge is here expounding the Hegelian concept of "grace."

2. There is a tradition within Kierkegaard scholarship to simply assume that the Judge's views are more acceptable to Kierkegaard than those of A. I am obviously not in agreement with this view.

3. See Thomas Merton's discussion of St. John of the Ladder in his *Disputed Questions* (New York: Farrar, Straus and Cudahy, 1953), ch. 3.

4. The correspondence between the view of women of the Judge and of the Seducer was pointed out by Louis Mackey, *Kierkegaard: A Kind of Poet* (Philadelphia: University of Pennsylvania Press, 1971), ch. 3.

5. A fine account of the Hegelian background of Strauss' views and of the controversy surrounding the publication of *The Life of Jesus* is found in W. J. Brazill, *The Young Hegelians* (New Haven: Yale University Press, 1970), ch. 3.

6. Quoted in H. C. Wolf, *Kierkegaard and Bultmann: The Quest for the Historical Jesus* (Minneapolis: Augsburg, 1965), p. 29.

7. Quoted in S. Crites' fine article "Pseudonymous Authorship as Art and as Act," in J. Thompson, ed., *Kierkegaard: A Collection of Critical Essays* (New York: Doubleday, 1972), p. 204.

Chapter Eight:
Two-Dimensional Life Patterns

1. The concept of *absolute telos* is very similar to Paul Tillich's later concept of *ultimate concern.*

2. This point is made in Mackey, *Kierkegaard*, p. 97.

3. For the problem of distinguishing a religious from a secular mode of existence, see the brilliant set of studies by Mircea Eliade, a good introduction to which is his *The Sacred and the Profane* (New York: Harper and Row, 1959).

4. Quoted from L. Dupre, *Kierkegaard as Theologian* (New York: Sheed and Ward, 1963), p. 171.

INDEX